At Risk

Earthquakes and Tsunamis on the West Coast

Kwakwaka'wakw earthquake mask (page 11)

At Risk

Earthquakes and Tsunamis on the West Coast

John Clague
Chris Yorath
Richard Franklin
Bob Turner

TRICOUNI PRESS
VANCOUVER

Library and Archives Canada Cataloguing in Publication

At risk : earthquakes and tsunamis on the West Coast / John Clague ... [et al.].

Includes bibliographical references and index.
ISBN 0-9697601-7-5

1. Earthquake hazard analysis—British Columbia—Pacific Coast.   2. Earthquake hazard analysis—Washington (State)—Pacific Coast.   3. Tsunamis—British Columbia—Pacific Coast.   4. Tsunamis—Washington (State)—Pacific Coast.   5. Earthquake prediction—British Columbia—Pacific Coast.   6. Earthquake prediction—Washington (State)—Pacific Coast. I. Clague, J. J. (John Joseph), 1946–

QE535.A84 2006   363.34'95'0971131   C2006-901104-4

Available from:
Tricouni Press Ltd.
3649 West 18th Avenue
Vancouver, BC, Canada V6S 1B3
Phone and fax: 604-224-1178
Email: books@tricounipress.com

and from Gordon Soules Book Publishers Ltd.

In Canada:
1359 Ambleside Lane
West Vancouver, BC, Canada V7T 2Y9
Phone: 604-922-6588 or 604-688-5466
Fax: 604-688-5442
Email: books@gordonsoules.com

In the United States:
PMB 620, 1916 Pike Place #12
Seattle, WA 98101-1097 USA
Phone: 604-922-6588 or 604-688-5466
Fax: 604-688-5442
E-mail: books@gordonsoules.com

Edited, designed, and typeset by Glenn and Joy Woodsworth
Set in Minion and Scala Sans
Cover designed by Richard Franklin; cover land image created by Robert Kung
Printed and bound in Canada by Friesens

Grants from the Canadian Geological Foundation and Simon Fraser University are gratefully acknowledged.

Dedicated to W.G. (Bill) Milne (1921–2005), the first director of the Geological Survey of Canada's Pacific Geoscience Centre and one of the most respected seismologists in North America.

Contents

Earthquakes with More than 10,000 Deaths since 1900

Date	Location	Deaths	Magnitude
April 4, 1905	Kangra, India	19,000	8.6
August 17, 1906	Valparaiso, Chile	20,000	8.2
October 21, 1907	Central Asia	12,000	8.1
December 28, 1908	Messina, Italy	70,000 to 100,000	7.2
January 13, 1915	Avezzano, Italy	29,980	7.5
February 1918	Kwangtung, China	10,000	7.3
December 16, 1920	Gansu, China	200,000	8.6
January 17, 1921	Bali, Indonesia	15,000	
September 1, 1923	Kanto, Japan	143,000	7.9
May 22, 1927	Tsinghai, China	200,000	7.9
December 25, 1932	Gansu, China	70,000	7.6
August 25, 1933	China	10,000	7.4
January 15, 1934	Bihar, India	10,700	8.1
May 30, 1935	Quetta, Pakistan	30,000 to 60,000	7.5
January 25, 1939	Chillan, Chile	28,000	8.3
December 26, 1939	Erzincan, Turkey	30,000	7.8
October 5, 1948	Ashgabat, Turkmenistan	110,000	7.3
February 29, 1960	Agadir, Morocco	10,000 to 15,000	5.7
September 1, 1962	Qazvin, Iran	12,230	7.3
August 31, 1968	Iran	12,000 to 20,000	7.3
January 4, 1970	Yunnan Province, China	10,000	7.5
May 31, 1970	Peru	66,000	7.9
May 10, 1974	China	20,000	6.8
February 4, 1975	China	10,000	7.0
February 4, 1976	Guatemala	23,000	7.5
July 28, 1976	Tangshan, China	255,000 to 655,000	7.5
September 16, 1978	Iran	15,000	7.8
September 19, 1985	Michoacan, Mexico	9,500 to 30,000	8.0
December 7, 1988	Spitak, Armenia	25,000	6.8
June 20, 1990	Western Iran	40,000 to 50,000	7.7
August 17, 1999	Turkey	17,118	7.6
January 26, 2001	India	20,023	7.7
December 26, 2003	Southeastern Iran	26,200	6.6
December 26, 2004	South Asia	300,000	9.3
October 8, 2005	Pakistan	86,000	7.6

Source: U.S. Geological Survey (http://earthquake.usgs.gov/regional/world/world_deaths.php).

Preface

IT IS ELEVEN MINUTES past two on a sunny Thursday afternoon in spring. Offices and classrooms throughout the Pacific Northwest are full. Malls are crowded. Ships of all sizes ply the harbours, carrying goods to and from the huge rail yards that line the shores. Airports are busy, their long, sleek runways like welcoming fingers to landing aircraft arriving from near and far. Highways are buzzing. Across suspension bridges, through tunnels, and under overpasses, many thousands of cars rush people to and from appointments. The cores of the larger cities are crowded with people, and tourists are beginning to arrive in the small coastal communities.

Suddenly, the world changes as the ground begins to move violently. From Vancouver Island to northern California, the floor of the Pacific Ocean moves upward 10 metres as the fault at the west edge of the North American continent unzips to the south at a speed of about 3 kilometres per second. Shockwaves move inland, and, at the same time, a tsunami races across the Pacific towards Asia and eastward towards the shores of Vancouver Island, Washington, Oregon, and California.

The violent shaking seems to go on forever. Loose objects crash to the ground, cars collide, and buildings collapse. Suspension bridges writhe like snakes and some tunnels cave in. Water mains break, gas lines rupture, and fires pop up everywhere. The ground cracks and subsides on deltas, river plains, and in landfill areas as loose, saturated sands liquefy. Some airports are damaged, and landslides block highways and rail lines in mountain valleys. About fifteen minutes after the shaking stops, the tsunami slams into the coast. Eerily, the sea pulls back from the shore moments before the first wave arrives and overwhelms everything as it rushes inland. The second and third waves are even bigger. The water returns to the sea, carrying houses, trees, and cars. And many lifeless bodies.

Hospitals and other medical facilities are swamped. Supplies and emergency aid are delayed because most airports, highways, and rail lines are inoperative. Over the course of the next week, fire crews and other rescue personnel will clear away debris, looking for survivors and the dead. Police will try to control widespread looting until the military arrives. Food, tents, and blankets will slowly trickle into cities and towns, but distribution will be hampered by damage to harbours and road systems.

Seismologists of the Geological Survey of Canada and the United States Geological Survey establish a magnitude of 9.3 for the earthquake, the same size as the quake that struck South Asia on December 26, 2004, and similar in magnitude to the one that happened in the Pacific Northwest on January 26, 1700. Another probably will happen in some 500 to 600 years. And yet despite the destruction and death, our cities and towns will be rebuilt. People will go on with their lives and, within a few decades, the memory of the "Big One" in Cascadia will fade.

The foregoing events are fictional, but at some future time a gigantic earthquake *will* strike the region, damaging its economy and leaving large numbers of people injured and dead. Some communities will suffer more than others. Larger cities, such as Vancouver, Victoria, Seattle, and Portland, will sustain localized but significant damage, whereas damage to some low-lying outer coastal communities like Astoria and Tofino may be catastrophic.

In the pages that follow, we explain the scientific underpinnings of earthquakes and their destructive effects. We focus on quakes of gigantic size that occur along the west coast of North America from central Vancouver Island to northern California. Our purpose is not to alarm people but to inform. We explain the science behind the assertions of geophysicists and geologists that a "Big One" will happen sometime in the next few hundred years. We look at geological and geophysical data that confirm the occurrence of these past events and show that they are caused by the periodic, sudden slippage of two of the Earth's tectonic plates. We also examine the possibility that large, damaging quakes occur along other kinds of faults, some of which pass through or near our cities. Although we discuss aspects of the subject that apply to the entire Pacific Northwest, our main focus is western British Columbia and Washington.

John Clague and Chris Yorath wrote the text and chose the photographs. Richard Franklin and Bob Turner created the graphics. Technical terms are flagged in bold face type where first used and are defined in the glossary. Sources of additional information and reading are given at the end of the book.

Kwakwaka'wakw earthquake mask used in ceremonial dances. According to Kwakwaka'wakw beliefs, the Earth is held in place with strong ropes held by a giant supernatural being. Earthquakes occur when the ropes slip from his grasp or when he moves his hands to get a better grip. Several ceremonial groups had this supernatural being as their patron. Earthquakes were portrayed in a series of dances whenever tremors were felt. The mask has a visor and lips, both of which can be moved by pulling a cord. The visor tips down over the eyes, which are inlaid with amber glass. Ropes were placed beneath the plank bench on which guests sat. When the mask appeared, men pulled the ropes back and forth, causing the bench to move. At the same time, earthquake-like noises were made. These acts illustrated the presence of the earthquake and the power of the mask, as well as displaying hereditary family privileges. The mask was made by John Davis at Kingcome Inlet, British Columbia, probably in the nineteenth century. It was last used at a potlatch in 1916.

THE VANCOUVER SUN

www.vancouversun.com   FINAL   THURSDAY, MARCH 1, 2001

Richter 6.8

'The magnitude of this quake is a wake-up call to B.C.'

ANTHONY P. BOLANTE/REUTERS

The serious damage in Wednesday's earthquake took place south of the border. Here, Kristi Heim of Seattle reacts outside the Starbucks corporate headquarters building in downtown Seattle.

Earthquakes are a serious hazard in the Pacific Northwest. The most recent large earthquake in the region, in February 2001, was centred near Nisqually, Washington, and caused about $2 billion damage (2006 dollars).

Shake, Rattle and Roll
Introduction

*Fate, whimsy, ignorance, sheer will – any number of things conspire
to put a city where it is. Once it's there, and it's big enough, it's there
forever. But if it's in an earthquake zone, you've created a civilization
that becomes drastically expensive to maintain...*
— Marc Reisner, *A Dangerous Place* (2003, p. 180)

EARTHQUAKES ARE ONE of the greatest natural hazards humans
face. During the twentieth century alone, over two million
people died during a total of less than thirty minutes of strong
ground shaking, attendant fires, tsunamis, and landslides. In
December 2003, the ancient city of Bam in Iran was destroyed by
an earthquake, with the loss of over 26,000 lives. One of the worst
disasters in modern times occurred in China in July 1976, when an
entire city was destroyed and over 200,000 people were killed in less
than six minutes. Earlier, in 1556, an earthquake in north-central
China killed an estimated 830,000 people. And most recently, first
on December 26, 2004, and later on October 8, 2005, close to
400,000 people in fourteen countries lost their lives to the effects of
large earthquakes off the west coast of Sumatra in Indonesia and in
northern Pakistan.

Some famous cities of antiquity, such as Alexandria, Corinth,
and the Bronze Age cities of Troy, Mycenae, and Knossos, were
partially to totally destroyed by earthquakes. The great city of
Harappa in the Indus Valley was likewise destroyed sometime after
2000 BC, ending its dominance in the region. And in the Holy Land,

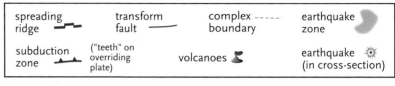

| spreading ridge | transform fault | complex boundary - - - - - | earthquake zone |
| subduction zone | ("teeth" on overriding plate) | volcanoes | earthquake (in cross-section) |

The Pacific Ring of Fire is a zone of intense earthquake and volcanic activity ringing the Pacific Ocean. The coastal Pacific Northwest and Chile lie within this zone. These two areas, and others along the Ring of Fire, are subduction zones, where the Pacific plate moves beneath a series of continental plates. Magma wells up (white arrows) beneath the spreading ridges, cools to form oceanic crust, and moves away from the spreading ridges towards subduction zones.

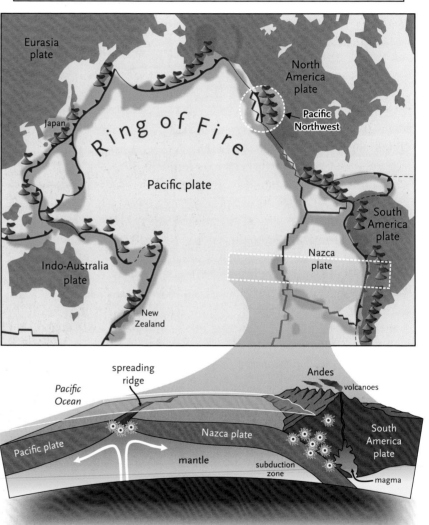

the ancient cities of Megiddo and Jericho, lying along one of Earth's great fault systems that extends from the Red Sea along the Dead Sea rift valley, were destroyed by earthquakes.

The cities of the Pacific Northwest, including Vancouver, Victoria, Seattle, Tacoma, Olympia, and Portland, lie within one of the world's great zones of earthquakes and active volcanoes, the so-called **Pacific Ring of Fire**. Two large and one small **crustal plates** interact with one another off the Pacific coast from Alaska to California, creating enormous forces deep below the surface. The **Pacific** and **North America plates** slowly slide past each other along two **faults**, the San Andreas fault in California and the **Queen Charlotte fault** off the coast of the Queen Charlotte Islands.

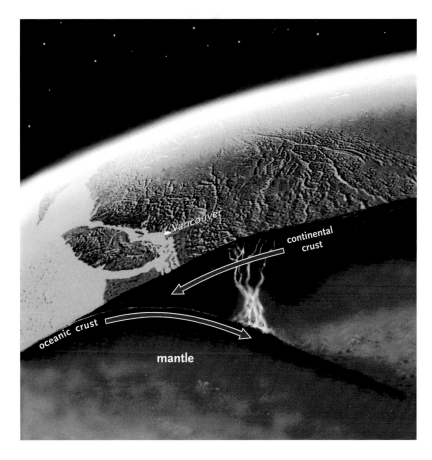

Artist's rendition of subduction of the oceanic Juan de Fuca plate beneath the continental North America plate.

Between these two faults, the small, oceanic **Juan de Fuca plate** descends beneath North America by a process earth scientists refer to as **subduction**. The boundary between the two converging plates is the **Cascadia subduction zone**; earthquakes as large as any on Earth have occurred along it. Interactions among these plates over the past 170 million years have created the mountains of western North America, the volcanoes of the Cascade Range, and the faults that riddle the western part of the continent.

Earth scientists have shown that subduction is a stick-slip process. Slip occurs in discrete episodes, hundreds of years apart, along the fault separating the North America and Juan de Fuca plates. This sudden movement produces a great earthquake of **magnitude** (M) 8 to 9+, much like the one that occurred in Alaska in 1964 (M 9.2) – the largest recorded quake in North America. One of a similar magnitude happened off our coast in January 1700, nearly 100 years before Captain James Cook entered Nootka Sound. At that time, a few tens of thousands of native people lived on the Cascadia coast, and today their descendants retain oral traditions of that – and other – large earthquakes. In the relatively short period since early European exploration, our west coast cities were established and grew to their present size. Much of this growth occurred without the benefit of current scientific knowledge of earthquakes. Regrettably, this has put some 10 million people and the economic wealth of the entire region in considerable jeopardy.

The megathrust fault is located offshore, below the ocean floor and at considerable depth beneath the edge of the continent, but geologists have identified other kinds of faults closer to and within our cities that may be storing energy to be released during future quakes. Examples include the Leech River fault, which passes through Victoria, and the Seattle fault, running through Seattle. Although smaller than the expected "Big One," some of these earthquakes will pack the punch of the cataclysmic 1995 quake at Kobe, Japan (M 6.9), which killed over 5500 people and caused damage estimated at $200 billion. How can we be sure of this? We know because such earthquakes have happened in this region during the past 150 years. For example, an earthquake beneath central Vancouver Island in 1946 had a magnitude of 7.3, larger than the Kobe earthquake, and another quake of similar magnitude struck north-central Washington in 1872. Most recently, in February 2001, a magnitude 6.9 quake hit the southern Puget Lowland near Olympia. Although property damage from some of these events was significant, had any of them been centred on a fault within one of our principal cities, the damage and suffering would have been much greater.

In his recent book *Dangerous Places,* Marc Reisner described how Los Angeles and San Francisco were established in one of the most earthquake-prone areas in the world. Developers and officials gave no thought to the inevitability of the rare, hard blows that Nature would deliver to these cities in the form of earthquakes. It happened in San Francisco in 1906 and 1989, and in Los Angeles in 1935, 1971, and 1994. Yet, San Francisco in particular has been rather lucky, for the 1906 earthquake (M 7.9) occurred when the population in the San Francisco Bay area was only about 400,000, small compared to the 6 million of today, and the **epicentre** of the 1989 earthquake was about 100 kilometres south of the city. Reisner speculated what would happen if a magnitude 7 earthquake occurred today on one of the many active faults within the metropolitan San Francisco-Oakland area. His musings are not for the faint of heart. Yet this earthquake is inevitable – scientists just can't say when or exactly where it will strike. The earthquake threat in the Pacific Northwest arises from a different cause than in California, but Reisner's comments about the concentration of people and wealth in dangerous places are pertinent to residents of Cascadia.

One hundred and fifty years ago, fewer than 50,000 people lived in the Pacific Northwest. Today the number is nearly two hundred times as great. Since that

San Francisco after the great 1906 earthquake. Much of the damage to the city resulted from fires triggered by the quake.

time, ten magnitude 6 or larger earthquakes have struck the region. When the population was small and scattered among widely separated communities, earthquakes were of little concern to governments, partly due to ignorance but also because earthquake damage and suffering were limited. Today, however, areas that are uninhabited or support only small populations are disappearing in the face of rapid urban growth. We are setting ourselves up for an earthquake that may cause great property damage and injure or kill large numbers of people.

Our goal in this book is to provide an understanding of earthquakes and seismic risk in the coastal Pacific Northwest. Our geographic focus is southwestern British Columbia and western Washington, and Oregon, which are adjacent to the Cascadia subduction zone. We do not discuss the causes of earthquakes in California, because their causes are different and because the California situation is handled admirably by many other authors (see Want More Information? on page 173). Although no one can say when or where the next earthquake will strike, the past gives us clues as to what to expect. It gives us a good idea of the probability, location, and consequences of future quakes of different magnitudes. From such information, we can infer the probable damage from strong earthquakes to Pacific Northwest communities.

Neptune,
Lord of the Earthquake
Plate tectonics

We learn geology the morning after the earthquake, on ghastly diagrams of cloven mountains, upheaved plains, and the dry bed of the sea.

— Ralph Waldo Emerson, *The Conduct of Life* (1860)

UNTIL THE EIGHTEENTH CENTURY, earthquakes were the subject of myth and philosophy. Their rational understanding, rooted in science, only began to develop at that time. The above quote from Ralph Waldo Emerson suggests a lingering contempt for earthquake science, perhaps in the hope that if one doesn't think about earthquakes, they will go away. Greeks in the eighth century BC believed that the god Poseidon was responsible for them, and later the Romans put the blame on their equivalent god Neptune. In the fourth century BC, the great Greek philosopher Aristotle argued for a natural cause, suggesting they resulted from subterranean winds inhaled into the Earth's crust during dry periods of calm weather, sometimes augmented by the appearance of comets. Similar fanciful ideas were subsequently held by popes, poets, and philosophers, most of whom fatalistically accepted the phenomenon as part of life, then got on with their day.

Following the devastating Lisbon earthquake of 1775, the German mathematician and philosopher Immanuel Kant wrote three treatises on the subject, rejecting William Whiston's then-popular comet theory. He proposed that earthquakes were due to subterranean caves that he thought were oriented parallel to mountain ranges and large rivers and that carry winds over long distances. Unlike Aristotle, however, he didn't stop at wind as a cause, but presumed that a mixture of two parts vitriol, eight parts water, and two parts iron would produce enough steam and flames to trigger an earthquake within his cave systems. From these musings, Kant deduced that houses and streets should never be built parallel to mountains and rivers.

Scientific study of earthquakes began in the nineteenth century and intensified in the first half of the twentieth century with studies of the 1906 San Francisco earthquake and the development of instruments capable of recording quakes. With modern instruments, **seismologists** are now able to pinpoint and characterize even small earthquakes with extraordinary precision, and the development of the theory of **plate tectonics** in the 1960s finally allowed scientists to understand their causes and distributions. A full description of plate tectonics is beyond the scope of this book. Suffice it to say that the theory has revolutionized earth science, enabling scientists from around the world to better understand why and how earthquakes occur. This chapter summarizes some of the results of their research.

The outermost shell of the Earth, or **crust**, is divided into eight large, independently moving fragments, or plates, and many smaller ones. Some plates include continents, whereas others are made entirely of oceanic crust. The cores of our continents, or **shields**, have been around for billions of years. They formed when the once-molten Earth cooled and individual pieces of primitive crust amalgamated into large fragments of continental size. The Canadian Shield of central Canada, for example, consists of several very different pieces of crust that assembled to form the North American continent about 1700 million years ago. Paul Hoffman, a geologist at Harvard University, once referred to this assemblage as "The United Plates of America." Thick blankets of **sedimentary rocks** have since accumulated on the Canadian Shield, and several additional pieces of crust have become welded to its edges to form the continent we know today.

The differences between continental and oceanic crust are substantial. Continental crust is thicker and lighter than the crust forming the ocean basins. The crust beneath North America is

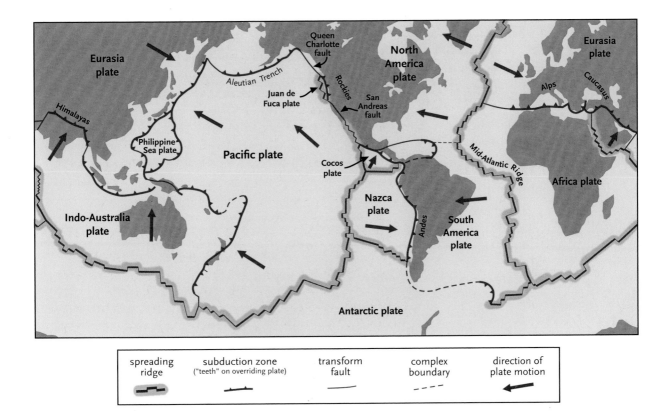

| spreading ridge | subduction zone ("teeth" on overriding plate) | transform fault | complex boundary | direction of plate motion |

about 40 kilometres thick and is dominated by rocks rich in light (low density) minerals such as **quartz** and **feldspar** that contain abundant silicon, aluminum, sodium, and potassium. Oceanic crust averages about 7 kilometres thick and contains denser minerals such as **pyroxene**, rich in magnesium and iron. Because of these differences, the continents float high, like icebergs, on the underlying **mantle**, whereas oceanic crust floats lower and forms the floors of the deep ocean basins.

Oceanic crust forms through the process of **seafloor spreading**. Molten rock, called **magma,** rises upward from the mantle along networks of fractures beneath **mid-ocean ridge** systems. Upon approaching the ocean floor, the magma rapidly cools and sticks to the walls of the fractures, forming vertical sheets or **dykes**. Some of the molten rock erupts onto the ocean floor to instantly solidify as

The Earth's crust is divided into eight large and many small, independently moving plates that interact with one another to produce earthquakes, volcanoes, and mountains.

In the northeast Pacific, new oceanic crust is created by upwelling of basaltic magma along fractures beneath Juan de Fuca Ridge. The newly formed crust moves away from the ridge, forming the trailing edges of the Pacific and Juan de Fuca plates.

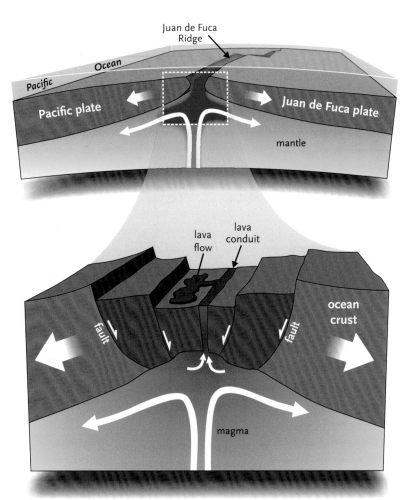

pillow basalt, a type of volcanic rock with large, pillow-like structures. With each succeeding injection of magma, the ocean crust spreads symmetrically away from the ridge. Through these processes, oceanic crust constantly grows and becomes systematically older away from the **spreading ridges**. If seafloor spreading were the only process operating, the Earth would get progressively larger over time, like a slowly inflating balloon. We know, however, that our planet has not changed much in size for many hundreds of millions of years. What, then, happens to the oceanic crust?

A look at a map of the Pacific Ocean with the water stripped

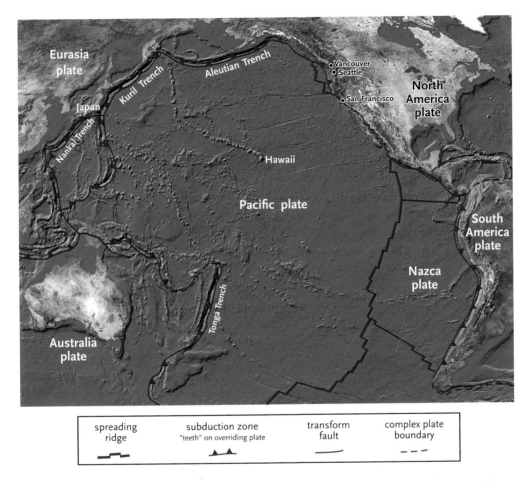

spreading ridge	subduction zone "teeth" on overriding plate	transform fault	complex plate boundary

away reveals the presence of long, narrow trenches along the margins of Asia and North and South America. It is beneath these trenches, in what are called **subduction zones**, that spreading ocean crust is consumed. Oceanic crust descends, or subducts, in a conveyor-belt fashion into the Earth's mantle from which it originated. This massive recycling process allows the planet to retain its size and also permits the plates to move relative to one another. Subduction of oceanic crust also accounts for the presence of chains of volcanoes, called **volcanic arcs**, inland of deep-sea trenches. The volcanoes occur on the overriding plate, above the subducting crust, their location depending on where the

The floor of the Pacific Ocean as it would appear with the water removed. The trenches at the edges of the Pacific are the sites where oceanic crust subducts beneath the adjacent continents. Note that the continents, which are underlain by relatively light crust, are elevated above the ocean floor, which is formed of denser crust.

Plate tectonic environment of British Columbia, Washington, and the adjacent Pacific Ocean, showing plate interactions and active volcanoes of the Cascade volcanic chain. In this view, ocean water has been removed to show features on the sea floor. The continental shelf, which is the light grey area east of the Queen Charlotte fault and the Cascadia subduction zone, is part of the North America plate, even though it is under water. The Cascade volcanoes are products of subduction of oceanic crust beneath western North America.

The two heavy green arrows show the direction of convergence of the Juan de Fuca plate with the North America plate. The Juan de Fuca plate is moving down to the east under North America. The volcanoes lie above the zone where water, driven from the descending plate, causes the overlying mantle to partially melt. The molten material then rises to erupt at the surface. The heavy red arrows indicate directions where plates are pulling apart at oceanic ridges. The thin red arrows indicate directions of relative motion where plates are sliding past one another. See page 15 for another view of these processes.

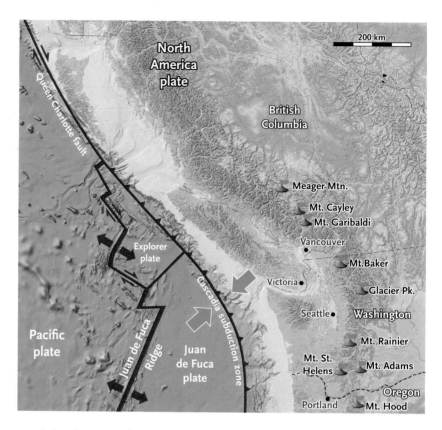

subducting crust becomes hot enough for the fluids escaping from it to partially melt the enclosing mantle. The buoyant molten material, magma, rises upward through the mantle and overlying crust to erupt at the surface. Repeated eruptions over a period of millions of years have created the Pacific volcanic arcs, including those of the Aleutian Islands, Andes, and Cascades, the last extending from southwestern British Columbia to northern California.

Earth's crustal plates move relative to one another in three ways. Two plates symmetrically diverge along spreading ridges as new oceanic crust is formed. Plates converge at subduction zones, where one plate is consumed beneath the other. In some areas, plates move horizontally past one another along what are called **transform faults**. The San Andreas fault in California, which separates the North America and Pacific plates, is a transform fault.

Mt. St. Helens with Mt. Rainier in the distance, photo taken November 12, 2004. The two mountains are active volcanoes, although Mt. Rainier has not erupted in historic time. Mt. St. Helens erupted explosively in May 1980 and has been restless ever since.

It extends northward from the East Pacific Rise, a spreading ridge in the southeast Pacific Ocean, through the Gulf of California, coming onshore just south of the Imperial Valley in California. The fault trace lies east of Los Angeles and just west of San Francisco. Residents of Los Angeles live on the Pacific plate, whereas most of those in San Francisco live on the North America plate. The Pacific plate is moving northward relative to the North America plate at an average rate of about five centimetres per year. Thus, in 11 million years, San Francisco will be a suburb of Los Angeles, or vice versa, depending on your preference! There are many transform faults throughout the world, along which pieces of crust are moving past one another. The mid-ocean ridges are segmented by transform faults, some of which extend great distances

Boundaries between crustal plates are of three types: transform plate boundaries along which adjacent plates move horizontally past one another, convergent plate boundaries where one plate is consumed beneath another, and divergent plate boundaries where new oceanic crust is created.

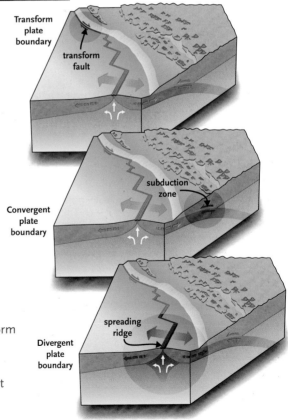

Different places, different quakes

Both California and the Pacific Northwest have strong earthquakes, but the quakes are different due to the nature of plate interactions in the two areas. In California, the Pacific and North America plates are sliding horizontally past one another along the San Andreas fault, which extends through the state from the Imperial Valley in the south to San Francisco in the north. Earthquakes on the San Andreas fault and on secondary faults associated with it result from sudden lateral slip of the crust (strike-slip earthquakes). Many quakes on other California faults result from vertical slip (dip-slip earthquakes).

In the Pacific Northwest, the Pacific and North America plates are separated by the Juan de Fuca plate, which is moving towards and beneath the continent. The fault bounding the Juan de Fuca and North America plates extends beneath the Pacific coast but not through the continent as the San Andreas fault does. Earthquakes on this landward-dipping fault stem from sudden westward shifts of North America over oceanic crust (**thrust earthquakes**, a specific type of dip-slip event). These earthquakes are huge but infrequent, and their **epicentres** are offshore and thus farther from cities and towns than epicentres on the San Andreas fault. Other, smaller but still very damaging earthquakes occur along faults that cut the crust of North America. The faults extend in an easterly direction across the Willamette Valley of northern Oregon, the Puget trough of western Washington, and the southern Strait of Georgia and Fraser Valley of British Columbia. Most of these quakes are dip-slip events.

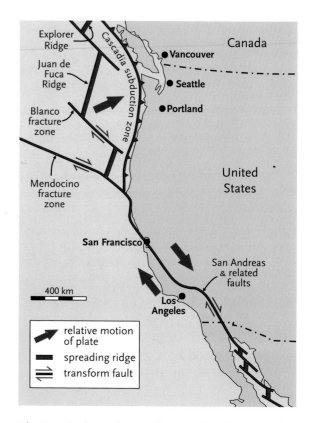

The San Andreas fault is the boundary between the North America and Pacific plates. The two plates are sliding slowly past one another along this fault. Farther north, the Juan de Fuca plate dives beneath the North America plate at the Cascadia subduction zone. California and the Pacific Northwest thus are characterized by very different types of plate boundaries and earthquakes.

into continents and are responsible for rift valleys such as the Dead Sea. Places where three different plates meet at a single point are called **triple junctions**. An example occurs off northwestern Vancouver Island, where the Pacific, **Explorer**, and North America plates meet at one point.

View northwest along the San Andreas fault in southern California where it crosses the Carrizo Plain. The fault separates the Pacific and North America plates and is the source of many large earthquakes in California.

trace of San Andreas fault

This book focuses on the Pacific Northwest, where the North America plate is separated by a fault from the much smaller, eastward-moving, oceanic Juan de Fuca plate. The Juan de Fuca plate is bordered on the north by the smaller Explorer plate along the **Nootka fault**. To the south, a similar fault separates the Juan de Fuca and **Gorda plates**. The Explorer and Gorda plates are breaking up as the North America plate overrides them.

The figure on page 29 shows the rates and directions of plate motions in the northeast Pacific relative to a stationary North America. The rates have been determined from magnetization of the ocean floor, as explained below, and are averages for time spans of thousands to millions of years. These rates do not apply, however, to intervals of hundreds of years, because the Juan de Fuca plate subducts in a series of massive, earthquake-generating jerks, each of which follows centuries of little relative plate motion when the Juan de Fuca plate is locked to North America.

How do we know how fast these plates are moving? Long before scientists formulated the theories of seafloor spreading and plate tectonics, it was discovered that the Earth's magnetic field periodically reverses – the north magnetic pole becomes the south magnetic pole and vice versa. The cause of the reversals lies within the Earth's **core** where the magnetic field originates. Fluid motions in the outer core produce a dynamo action as the Earth rotates about its axis. The motions in the core interact with the Earth's rotational motion in such a way that, occasionally, the magnetic field reverses. Past reversals in the magnetic field are known from studies of the magnetic properties of rocks on land whose ages are known. The studies have shown that rocks of the same age from

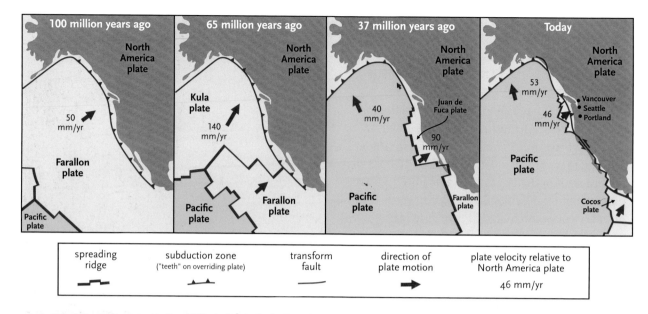

| spreading ridge | subduction zone ("teeth" on overriding plate) | transform fault | direction of plate motion | plate velocity relative to North America plate 46 mm/yr |

Plates of the past

The Juan de Fuca plate and its much larger predecessor, the **Farallon plate**, have been subducting beneath North America for about 175 million years, since the giant supercontinent known as **Pangea** broke up and created the Atlantic Ocean basin. Pangea included all of the world's continents, which had amalgamated due to plate motions about 300 million years ago. About 100 million years ago, when Vancouver Island became welded to North America, the Pacific Ocean floor consisted of one large, eastward-converging plate, the Farallon plate. About 15 million years later, a new spreading ridge developed, dividing the Farallon plate into two new separate plates. The northern, or **Kula, plate** moved northward and was ultimately consumed at the Aleutian Trench. All that remains of the Farallon plate is the small Juan de Fuca plate, which is converging towards the North America plate at a rate of 40 millimetres per year.

The huge oceanic Farallon plate split into two separate plates about 85 million years ago. The northern, Kula plate ultimately was entirely consumed by subduction beneath the Aleutian trench. The southern, Farallon plate bordered the Pacific plate along Juan de Fuca Ridge and continued to converge on North America. Today, all that remains of the Farallon plate is the tiny Juan de Fuca plate. The arrows show directions and rates of plate movement. The length of the arrows is proportional to plate velocity relative to the North America plate.

widely separated localities have the same polarity, whereas younger and older rocks have the opposite polarity. By piecing together the magnetic properties of rocks of many ages, scientists have established a global succession of normal and reversed polarity intervals.

So, what does this have to do with rates of

plate motions? Molten material from the mantle is injected into rifts beneath spreading ridges, where it cools and welds to the walls of the rifts. When the hot basalt cools to a certain temperature, the magnetic minerals in the rock become aligned with their poles parallel to the direction of the Earth's magnetic field. Like a tape recorder, the spreading oceanic crust faithfully records the polarity of the magnetic field as molten material is continuously injected into the mid-ocean ridge. In this manner, episodes of normal and reversed polarity are symmetrically recorded on both sides of the ridge along its entire length.

Instruments towed across the surface of the ocean can detect the magnetism of the rocks on ocean floor below. Such surveys have shown that the seafloor basalts are permanently magnetized in symmetrical, parallel stripes of normal and reversed polarity extending away from mid-ocean ridges. In 1961, Ronald Mason and Arthur Raff published the first magnetic map of the northeastern Pacific Ocean off Vancouver Island and Washington. The map clearly showed the parallel magnetic striping that quickly led scientists to the hypothesis of seafloor spreading (next page).

We know the age span of any given magnetic stripe on the ocean floor from the dated succession of normal and reversed polarity intervals worked out on land and also from dating seafloor rock samples obtained by ocean floor drilling. Knowing the ages of the stripes, it is easy to calculate the rate at which oceanic crust is spreading away from the ridge.

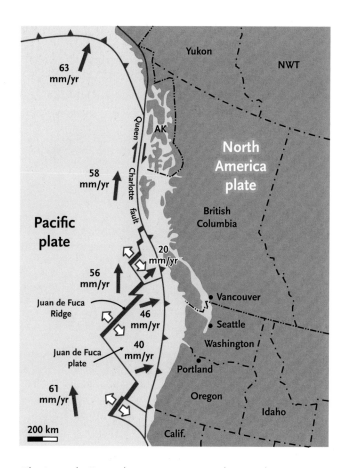

The Juan de Fuca plate converges on the North America plate at a rate of about 45 millimetres per year. Farther north, the Pacific plate moves past North America along the Queen Charlotte fault at about 58 millimetres per year. The red arrows show the directions of plate movement relative to North America. The white arrows indicate directions of seafloor spreading away from Juan de Fuca Ridge. The plate motions are responsible for most of the earthquakes in the Pacific Northwest.

Mason and Raff's 1961 map of the Earth's magnetic field in the eastern North Pacific Ocean, the "Rosetta Stone" of seafloor spreading and plate tectonics (top). The black stripes record intervals of normal magnetic polarity, like today, and the intervening blue stripes represent intervals when the Earth's magnetic field was reversed.

The bottom illustration shows the formation of the magnetic stripes by the conveyor-like movement of new crust away from the Juan de Fuca spreading ridge. The large red arrows indicate directions of plate movement away from the spreading ridge. The small red arrows are directions of motion along transform faults, which connect segments of the ridge.

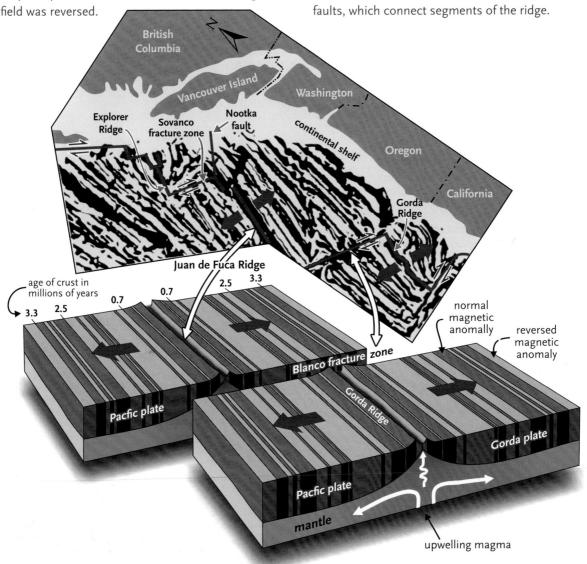

The Face of an Earthquake
A primer on seismology

We will probe for earthquakes, grub them up, and give vent to the dangerous gas.

— Henry David Thoreau, *Paradise (To Be) Regained* (1843)

Earthquakes are caused by sudden releases of energy that has accumulated along faults that cut the Earth's crust, analogous to energy that accumulates in a stout stick as it is bent. Faults are the "weak links" of the crust and will rupture when the accumulated energy finally exceeds their strength, much as a stick snaps when it is bent too much. Rocks on opposite sides of the fault move rapidly past one another, and the accumulated energy is released. The energy travels through the Earth and across its surface as **seismic waves**, similar to ripples moving away from the point where a pebble enters a pond.

When a fault breaks, the energy stored within the rocks is released instantly and moves away from the source like the shock wave from an explosion. The amount of released energy depends on two things – the distance of slip across the fault, measured in centimetres or metres, and the total area of the fault rupture. The latter ranges from about 100 square metres for the smallest recorded earthquakes to many thousands of

An earthquake is produced by the sudden displacement of rocks along a fault. The rupture of the rock sends out waves of vibration energy from the source.

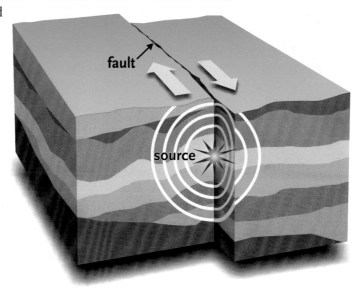

fault

source

31

square kilometres for a large one. The energy released during the 1960 Chile earthquake (M 9.5), the most powerful quake ever recorded, was greater than the total energy consumed annually in the United States and 10 million times greater than that of the Bikini atomic bomb detonation of 1946. **Seismographs** around the world recorded the Earth ringing like a bell for several weeks following the earthquake.

Shaking during an earthquake results from seismic waves of different types, frequencies, and velocities. As the waves move from one kind of earth material into another, their paths can be bent or reflected. Two separate waves may combine to produce a larger and more powerful wave. The type and intensity of the ground shaking depend on the dominant period of the seismic waves, which in turn depends on earthquake magnitude, distance from the epicentre, and the types of earth materials being shaken. Short-period (high-frequency) waves, which are most damaging to low structures such as houses and schools, rapidly diminish with increasing distance from the epicentre of a large earthquake. In contrast, long-period (low-frequency) waves are more damaging to tall buildings and long structures such as bridges and tunnels, and they travel much farther.

The net effect of all this, what people experience at the surface, is a mix of movements that commonly change during the shaking; to use a metaphor, a discordant symphony with blaring horns, shrieking violins, and an out-of-control conductor. The duration of shaking depends on the magnitude of the earthquake. A few tens of seconds of strong shaking are typical for a magnitude 7

Seismogram of the 1989 Loma Prieta, California, earthquake. The **period** (time between successive seismic waves) and **amplitude** (the height of the wave) varied during the earthquake. At this site in Norway, some 8400 kilometres from the epicentre of the earthquake, the first **P wave** (see page 37) arrived about 11 minutes before the first **S wave**.

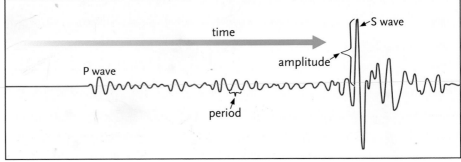

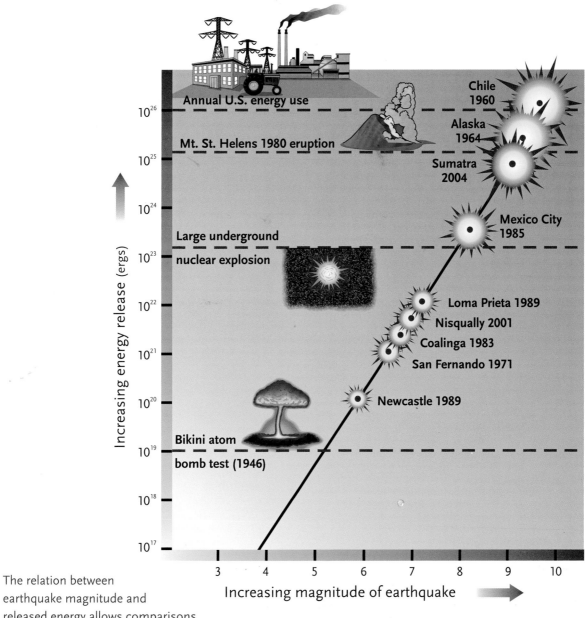

The relation between earthquake magnitude and released energy allows comparisons with other energy sources. The energy released by the 1960 earthquake in Chile, the most powerful historic seismic event, was greater than the entire annual U.S. consumption of commercial energy.

earthquake, whereas a magnitude 9 quake, like the one off Sumatra in December 2004, produces several minutes of strong shaking, what might seem like a lifetime to a person near its epicentre. For a very large earthquake, the duration of ground shaking may have a greater effect on structures than the magnitude of the earthquake itself. Most of the energy in very large earthquakes is carried in low-frequency, long-period waves. The relationship between earthquake magnitude and energy release is a **logarithmic** one, whereby a unit increase in magnitude, say from 2 to 3, corresponds to about a 30-fold increase of energy.

History of earthquake studies in the Pacific Northwest

The Milne seismograph, installed at Victoria in 1898, was the first instrument to record earthquakes in the Pacific Northwest. It recorded only large earthquakes and used a simple clock to mark time.

Scientists began to study earthquakes in the Pacific Northwest in 1898 when the first seismograph in the region was established at Victoria. This instrument recorded only strong, low-frequency (long-period) ground motions originating from earthquakes larger than magnitude 4.5. Fifty years later, the first sensitive, short-period seismographs came into operation, allowing smaller quakes to be recorded. As our understanding of the earthquake threat in British Columbia improved, the Canadian Government installed a large network of seismographs and strong ground motion instruments. The seismographs acquire data in electronic form and transmit them in real time to the Pacific Geoscience Centre, an office of the Geological Survey of Canada near Victoria. The modern seismograph network in southwestern British Columbia can detect earthquakes

Locations of operating seismic stations in the Pacific Northwest. The dense cluster of seismic stations in southern Washington monitors activity at Mt. St. Helens.

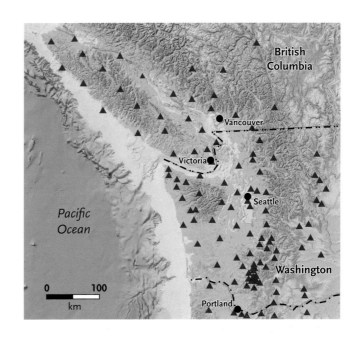

with magnitudes as low as 1.5 and can determine their epicentres to within 2 kilometres.

The first seismograph in Washington dates to 1906. Until the 1970s, scientists relied on the World-Wide Seismograph Station Network for locating earthquakes in Washington as small as magnitude 4. An extensive, sensitive seismic network was deployed in western Washington in the 1970s, and today earthquake epicentres can be pinpointed in that region to within 2 kilometres. The explosive eruption of Mount St. Helens in 1980 prompted installation of additional instruments in southern Washington and northern Oregon to assist in monitoring volcanic activity on the mountain.

The first studies designed to detect crustal deformation associated with earthquakes in British Columbia took place in the late 1970s. These studies included spirit-levelling and triangulation surveys, precise gravity measurements, and analysis of long-term trends in tidal records. Today, global positioning satellites (GPS) give highly precise measurements (within millimetres) of ground positions using continuous tracking sites. Crustal deformation studies in Washington have been conducted by the United States Geological Survey and

HERMAN® is reprinted with permission from LaughingStock Licensing Inc., Ottawa, Canada. All Rights Reserved.

Locations of GPS tracking stations (red dots) in the Pacific Northwest. Arrows show the direction and amount of horizontal crustal motion relative to a fixed reference station at Penticton, British Columbia. Longer arrows indicate faster motion.

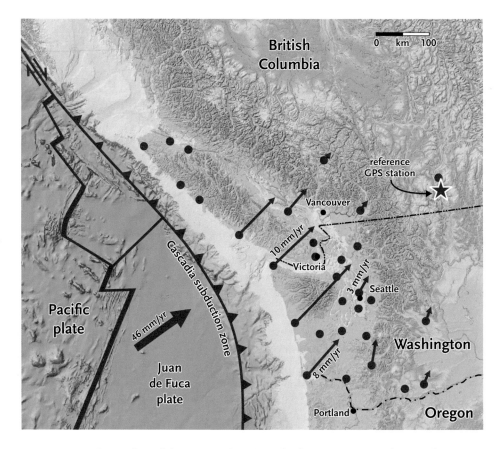

Central Washington University; the latter manages the Pacific Northwest Geodetic Array of continuous tracking stations. Together, the Canadian and American tracking networks have revolutionized earthquake hazard studies, making it possible to measure the ongoing crustal deformation responsible for large earthquakes.

With this impressive array of instruments, U.S. and Canadian seismologists record vertical and horizontal ground motions caused by earthquakes in the Pacific Northwest. Data are transmitted from seismographs directly to central computers via telephone lines, radio and microwave links, and satellites. Epicentres, **focal depths**, and magnitude can now be calculated from these data within minutes of an earthquake.

Seismic waves

Earthquakes generate three different types of waves. The first two types, called **body waves**, travel through the Earth. The faster of the two is the **compressional** or **P wave** (also called **primary wave**), which moves by pushing and pulling the rock or **sediment** in its path. An interesting feature of P waves is that, when they reach the Earth's surface, part of their energy is transmitted to the atmosphere as sound waves. That is why high-frequency P waves are occasionally heard as a distinctive bang, particularly during small earthquakes. The second type of body wave is the slower-moving **shear**, or **S wave**, which moves in a snake-like motion, perpendicular to the travel direction. The third type of seismic waves is **surface waves**. These waves are comparable to ripples travelling across a lake. Again, there are two types. **Love waves**, like S waves, move the ground from side to side, but they have no vertical motion. Love waves can be particularly damaging to the foundations of structures. Slower-moving **Rayleigh waves** are like rolling ocean waves; surface materials move vertically as the wave moves forward. If you are standing on a gravel driveway during an earthquake, you will first experience shaking caused by body waves. Then you may notice the swishing sound of the gravel and see it shift back and forth as the Love waves pass. A moment or two later, the ocean-like Rayleigh waves move through.

The epicentre of an earthquake is the position on the Earth's surface directly above the source or **focus** (or **hypocentre**) of the quake. The focus is the point on the fault surface where the rupture starts. Seismologists determine the epicentre and focus from the speeds at which earthquake waves travel through the Earth. The speed of P and S waves depends on

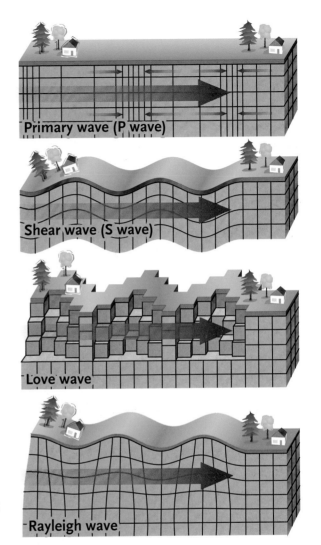

Earthquake waves are of four main types. Primary (P) waves are push-pull; shear (S) waves are like snapping a rope; Love waves whip the ground from side to side; and Rayleigh waves roll the ground like waves at sea. The large arrows indicate the direction of travel of the waves.

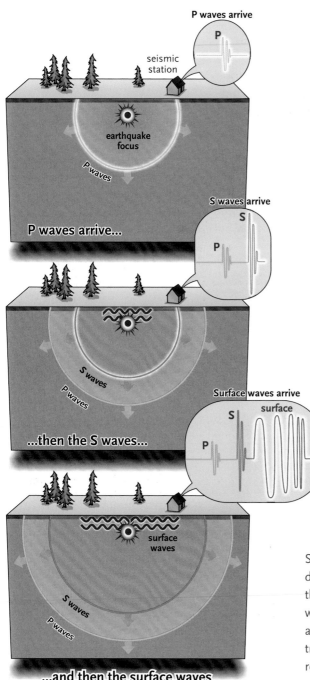

P waves arrive

P

seismic station

P waves arrive...

earthquake focus

P waves

S waves arrive

S

P

...then the S waves...

S waves

P waves

Surface waves arrive

surface

S

P

surface waves

...and then the surface waves

S waves

P waves

the density and elastic properties of the material through which they travel. For example, P waves travel through the Earth at velocities of 6 to 13 kilometres per second, whereas S waves are about 60 percent slower. Seismologists estimate velocities that best represent the crust of the Earth in their area, and from these calculate the travel times of P and S waves to a given seismograph. The interval between the arrivals of P and S waves depends on the distance from the focus to the seismograph. The epicentre is determined by measuring the differences in arrival times of P and S waves at three or more widely separated seismographs (diagram on facing page).

Most earthquakes occur in the crust at depths of less than 30 kilometres. However, in a few places, such as subduction zones, they occur at depths up to 700 kilometres. Focal depths can be determined in several ways. A common method is to identify on **seismograms** P and S waves that have been reflected back into the Earth from its surface at points near the epicentre. Such reflected waves have unique signatures and, at distant seismographs, follow the P waves by an interval that changes slowly with distance but rapidly with depth. If the distance between the epicentre

Seismic waves travel at different speeds and along different paths. P waves travel through the Earth and are the first to arrive at a seismic recording station. Slower S waves, which also travel through the Earth, arrive later and are followed by even slower surface waves, which travel along the Earth's surface. Each type of wave is recorded in succession by a seismograph.

and a nearby recording station is known, focal depth can be calculated from the time difference between the P and reflected P waves. Depths can likewise be determined from S wave arrivals.

A typical paper seismogram is shown on the next page. It records an earthquake of magnitude 3.9 that occurred on October 24, 1989, at a depth of about 35 kilometres within the Juan de Fuca plate beneath Barkley Sound on the west coast of Vancouver Island. The quake lasted for about two minutes, as shown by the time marks at the bottom of the record. The squiggly horizontal lines are marks left by a stylus as the paper, mounted on a drum, rotated beneath it. The time interval between the lines depends on the speed of the drum, which can be changed. Note the difference in the amplitude of the P wave at "P" and the S wave at "S." The long tail of waves trailing off to the right marks the surface (Rayleigh) waves. This seismogram was recorded at the Gonzales Observatory in Victoria and telemetred to the Pacific Geoscience Centre. Most seismic stations now use computers to record earthquakes; paper records have largely been discontinued.

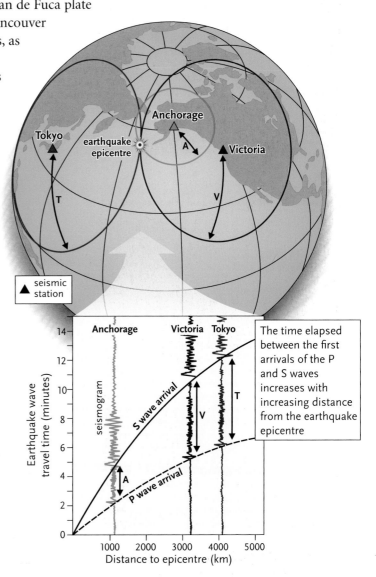

The epicentre of an earthquake can be determined from the arrival times of P and S waves at three or more widely separated sites. P and S waves travel at different velocities, and the times between the first arrivals of the P and S waves are proportional to the distance of the recording station from the earthquake epicentre. A circle with a radius equal to the epicentral distance is drawn around each seismograph station. The intersection of the three circles is the epicentre. The more stations that record the earthquake, the more precise its location.

The time elapsed between the first arrivals of the P and S waves increases with increasing distance from the earthquake epicentre

Drum seismographs provide excellent visual images of earthquakes. As the drum rotates once every 15 minutes, a pen records the movement of the ground.

This magnitude 3.9 earthquake was recorded on a drum seismograph located at the Gonzales Observatory in Victoria on October 24, 1989. Note the sharp arrival of the P waves at 3:54 PM. The stronger S waves arrive about 25 seconds later, after which the shaking gradually drops off.

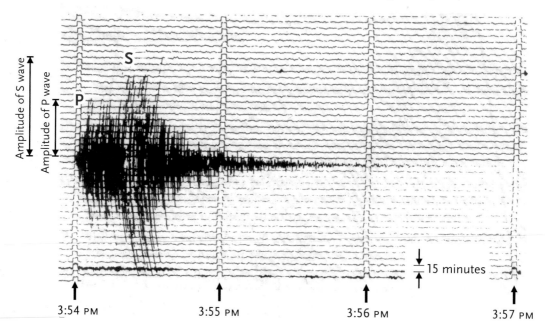

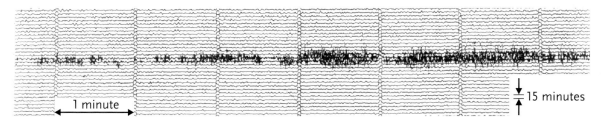

1 minute

15 minutes

The characteristic signature of an earthquake – a P wave followed by a higher-amplitude S wave – is clearly missing in the record at the top of this page, collected on January 11, 1996. This recording shows a series of irregular waves interrupted by periods of quiescence. The record came from a seismograph located on the grounds of the Port Alberni High School and was telemetred to the Pacific Geoscience Centre. Based upon his experience and the character of the recording, one of the seismic technicians thought that someone was trying to break into the concrete vault that housed the seismograph. He phoned the Port Alberni RCMP who promised to immediately investigate. A short time later, the technician received a return phone call reporting that a young couple was found *in flagrante delicto* on the roof of the seismic vault. To our knowledge, this is the world's only seismograph recording of an act of love.

This seismogram was recorded by a seismograph located in a vault on the grounds of the Port Alberni Secondary School on January 11, 1996. The repeated waxing and waning of energy and the lack of distinct P and S wave phases indicate that this event was not an earthquake. It was discovered that its cause was a young couple getting to know one another on the roof of the seismic vault.

Charles F. Richter (left) and Kiyoo Wadati (right). These renowned seismologists developed the first earthquake magnitude scales.

Earthquake magnitude

The magnitude of an earthquake is a quantitative measurement by which earthquakes can be compared world-wide. In 1931, the Japanese seismologist Kiyoo Wadati devised a scale that in 1935 was further developed by Charles F. Richter at the California Institute of Technology. The scale, somewhat to Richter's embarrassment, became known in the popular press as the

Measuring the size of earthquakes

The earthquake magnitude scale, first devised in 1931 by Japanese seismologist Kiyoo Wadati and modified in 1935 by Charles Richter, is a numerical scale of earthquake magnitude or strength. Magnitude on the so-called "Richter scale" is related to the amount of energy released during an earthquake and is determined by the largest amplitude of the shear wave, measured 100 kilometres from an earthquake epicentre on a standard seismograph. The amplitude is converted to a magnitude using logarithms – a magnitude 7 earthquake, for example, produces a displacement on a seismograph ten times larger than an earthquake of magnitude 6. However, the energy released, which is proportional to magnitude, is about 30 times greater. Thus, a magnitude 7 earthquake releases about 900 times (30 × 30) the energy of a magnitude 5 quake. Although there is no ceiling to the scale, the strength of earth materials and the lengths of the largest faults on Earth limit the actual maximum magnitude to about 9.5. Since the development of the Richter scale, several other scales have been created that provide similar, but not identical earthquake magnitude values. The m_b scale is derived from primary, or compressional, P waves, and the M_S scale from surface Love waves. The common practice today is to use a scale based on moment magnitude, M_W, which is based on the earthquake's seismic moment, defined as the product of the average amount of slip on the fault and the area that actually ruptured. As a rule of thumb, a magnitude nine earthquake is generated by a fault rupture about 1000 kilometres long. A moment magnitude 10 earthquake would require a 10,000-kilometre-long rupture whereas a magnitude 11 quake would require slippage on a fault that circles the Earth two and a half times; clearly such a magnitude is impossible on Earth.

Richter scale. It quantified the magnitude of local (California) earthquakes as the logarithm to the base 10 of the maximum signal wave amplitude recorded on a then-standard seismogram at a distance of 100 kilometres from the epicentre. By this scheme, the signal amplitude of earthquake waves increases 10 times for every unit increase in magnitude. The signal amplitude of an earthquake decreases as the distance from the focus increases. Richter developed a magnitude scale that compensates for this decrease in energy.

Several earthquake magnitude scales have been developed since Richter's time. The **local magnitude** scale, abbreviated M_L, is used mainly to characterize earthquakes with epicentres close to the recording station. It is based on the large-amplitude shear waves. For more distant events, compressional P-waves can be used to calculate a **body wave magnitude**, m_b. However, values of M_L and m_b are too small for large earthquakes. In such cases, the M_S scale, which is based on the amplitude of the largest Rayleigh waves, is more appropriate. The values of m_b and M_S are roughly equivalent for shallow, moderate-sized earthquakes, which are dominated by high-frequency waves. Neither measure, however, is appropriate for great earthquakes that occur along subduction zones. A further improvement in quantifying earthquake size was the development of what has been termed **moment magnitude**, M_w. First proposed in the 1960s by the Japanese-American seismologist Keiiti Aki, moment magnitude is defined as the product of the surface area of the fault and the amount of displacement along it. Today, common practice in the Pacific Northwest is to assign local magnitudes, M_L, to earthquakes less than magnitude 4 and moment magnitudes, M_W, to larger quakes. The Geological Survey of Canada now routinely adds a value of 0.62 to local magnitudes as low as 2.5 to provide moment magnitudes for offshore earthquakes. This adjustment is based on calibration studies between M_L and M_W.

Earthquake intensity

After a significant earthquake in the Pacific Northwest, questionnaires are sent to people living in the affected area. The answers to these questions enable seismologists to estimate the **intensity** of the earthquake and to construct an **isoseismal map** like the one prepared for the 1946 Vancouver Island earthquake by Garry Rogers, Chief Seismologist at the Geological Survey of Canada's Pacific Geoscience Centre. The contours that surround the epicentre define the distribution of intensity zones according to the **Modified Mercalli Intensity Scale**. Individual replies to such questionnaires can be highly subjective and variable, even within the same zone, but taken together, they give estimates of potential seismic hazards and useful information that can be applied in regional earthquake studies. Before the establishment of seismographs at Victoria and Seattle near the beginning of the last century, isoseismal maps based mainly on newspaper accounts were the only means by which the magnitudes of old earthquakes could be estimated. With the introduction of the Internet, maps of earthquake intensity can be generated from questionnaires completed on home computers.

Seismologist Garry Rogers

Mercalli Intensity Scale

Another measure of earthquake size is intensity. The intensity of an earthquake at any location depends on magnitude, distance from the epicentre, and the nature of the ground at the site. The Modified Mercalli Intensity Scale measures the degree to which an earthquake affects people, property, and the ground:

I   Not felt except by a very few under especially favourable circumstances.

II   Felt only by a few persons at rest, especially on upper floors of buildings. Delicately suspended objects may swing.

III   Felt quite noticeably indoors, especially on upper floors of buildings, but many people do not recognize it as an earthquake. Standing motor cars may rock slightly. Vibration like passing truck. Duration estimated.

IV   During the day felt indoors by many, outdoors by few. At night some awakened. Dishes, windows, doors disturbed; walls make creaking sound. Sensation like heavy truck striking building. Standing motor cars rock noticeably.

V   Felt by nearly everyone; many awakened. Some dishes, windows etc. broken; a few instances of cracked plaster; unstable objects overturned. Disturbances of trees, poles and other tall objects sometimes noticed. Pendulum clocks may stop.

VI   Felt by all; many frightened and run outdoors. Some heavy furniture moved; a few instances of fallen plaster or damaged chimneys. Damage slight.

VII   Everyone runs outdoors. Damage negligible in buildings of good design and construction; slight to moderate in well-built ordinary structures; considerable in poorly built or badly designed structures; some chimneys broken. Noticed by persons driving motor cars.

VIII   Damage slight in specially designed structures; considerable in ordinary substantial buildings, with

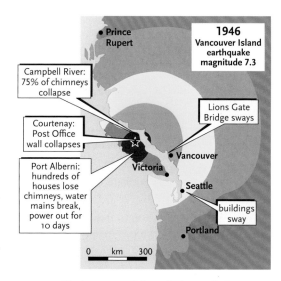

1946
Vancouver Island earthquake magnitude 7.3

Campbell River: 75% of chimneys collapse

Lions Gate Bridge sways

Courtenay: Post Office wall collapses

Port Alberni: hundreds of houses lose chimneys, water mains break, power out for 10 days

buildings sway

Prince Rupert • Vancouver • Victoria • Seattle • Portland

0   km   300

Shake maps (Mercalli intensity)

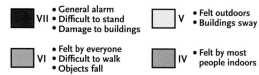

VII • General alarm • Difficult to stand • Damage to buildings

V • Felt outdoors • Buildings sway

VI • Felt by everyone • Difficult to walk • Objects fall

IV • Felt by most people indoors

2001
Nisqually, Washington earthquake magnitude 6.9

more than $2 billion in damage

Prince Rupert • Vancouver • Victoria • Seattle • Portland

0   km   300

Directions of fault motion during an earthquake

Seismologists can identify the direction of first motion along the rupture surface by noting the direction of compression and expansion, or dilation, of the P wave as it leaves the fault. A seismograph located at a site where the displaced rocks move closer to the instrument would record compression, whereas one at a site where the rocks move away would record extension. In this way, a seismologist can determine the type and orientation of the fault surface. The three main types of faults are (1) **wrench** or **strike-slip faults**, along which rocks move horizontally past one another; (2) **normal faults**, where one block drops relative to the other along a fault inclined toward the down-dropped block; and (3) **thrust faults**, where one block is shoved over the other block along a fault inclined downward toward the up-thrown block.

OPPOSITE: Modified Mercalli intensity maps for two earthquakes in the Pacific Northwest. The Nisqually earthquake was smaller than the Vancouver Island event, but it occurred in a highly populated region and caused much more damage.

partial collapse; great in poorly built structures. Panel walls thrown out of frame structures. Fall of chimneys, factory stacks, columns, monuments, walls. Heavy furniture overturned. Sand and mud ejected in small amounts. Changes in well water. Disturbs persons driving motor cars.

IX   Damage considerable in specially designed structures; well designed frame structures thrown out of plumb; great in substantial buildings, with partial collapse. Buildings shifted off foundations. Ground cracked conspicuously. Underground pipes broken.

X   Some well-built wooden structures destroyed; most masonry and frame structures destroyed with foundations; ground badly cracked. Rails bent. Landslides considerable from river banks and steep slopes. Shifted sand and mud. Water splashed over banks.

XI   Few, if any, (masonry) structures remain standing. Bridges destroyed. Broad fissures in ground. Underground pipelines completely out of service. Earth slumps and land slips in soft ground. Rails bent greatly.

XII   Damage total. Waves seen on ground surfaces. Lines of sight and level destroyed. Objects thrown upward into the air.

Intensity maps for earthquakes in the Pacific Northwest are now created with the help of the Internet. After an earthquake, people can access web pages of the Geological Survey of Canada and the U.S. Geological Survey to electronically submit forms detailing their experience. Earthquake intensity maps can be generated in a few minutes in the United States and in less than 24 hours in Canada. Efforts are currently underway to integrate the two systems. Additional maps, showing the intensity of ground shaking during earthquakes, are produced in a matter of minutes in the United States for the benefit of emergency managers. These maps are based on data from a large number of strong-motion seismographs. They show the areas of highest intensity, where damage is likely to be greatest. Canada has yet to develop a similar automated capability.

There are three types of faults. Normal faults involve extension, thrust faults compression, and strike-slip faults horizontal shear. The fault separating the Juan de Fuca and North America plates is a large thrust fault. The San Andreas fault is a strike-slip fault.

rock layers

fault line

Normal fault

tensile stress

fault plane

Thrust fault

compressive stress

Strike-slip fault

shear stress

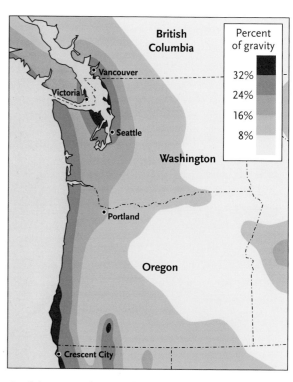

Peak horizontal ground accelerations with a 10% chance of occurring in the next fifty years. Ground acceleration is a measure of the intensity of earthquake shaking and is used by engineers to design safe buildings and other structures. The highest peak accelerations are in areas bordering the Strait of Georgia and Puget Sound and along the coast of southern Oregon.

Measuring ground motion

Two commonly asked questions about earthquakes are "How fast does the ground move?" and "How far does it move?" Ground velocities and accelerations can be measured with strong-motion seismographs, or **accelerometers**. These instruments are designed to operate close to an epicentre without being damaged or going off scale, allowing ground motions to be measured in the epicentral area during the period of strongest shaking. Ground accelerations are usually expressed as a percentage of the acceleration of gravity, which at sea level is about 980 centimetres per second per second. In other words, the velocity of an object will increase at a rate of 980 centimetres per second each second that it is in motion.

Measured accelerations a few tens of kilometres from the epicentre of a moderate to strong earthquake commonly range from 5 to 50% of gravity. A complication is that accelerations depend on the frequency of the seismic waves and the amount of ground displacement. For example, high-frequency waves of 10 cycles per second that displace the ground by 1 centimetre can have an acceleration of about 40% of gravity and be very damaging to small buildings. In contrast, low-frequency waves, slower

Earthquake ground motion and building codes

Earthquake ground motions are an important element of national and state building codes. The 1995 National Building Code of Canada includes **seismic zonation maps** prepared by the Geological Survey of Canada that show areas of the country with different expected peak ground accelerations and velocities. The coastal Pacific Northwest is the most seismically active region in Canada. The proposed 2005 National Building Code specifies that new buildings in Victoria should be constructed to withstand shaking with sustained peak horizontal ground accelerations of up to 34% of gravity. This acceleration has a 10% chance of occurring in a 50-year period. The new code also specifies accelerations at different wave periods to provide engineers with better estimates of shaking intensity than the traditional single peak ground acceleration value. These "spectral accelerations" have 2% chances of occurring in a 50-year period. Tall buildings are more vulnerable to low-frequency, long-period waves than low buildings. Conversely, low buildings are more affected by high-frequency, short-period waves. The building codes of the states of Washington, Oregon, and California differ only in detail from those of Canada. For example, in the mid 1970s the U.S. Applied Technology Council designated a peak ground acceleration of 20% of gravity at a 10% probability of being exceeded once in 50 years as the standard for building construction in northwestern Washington.

The 2005 version of the National Building Code of Canada is the first to take into account a great earthquake at the Cascadia subduction zone. The "design" subduction earthquake has a moment magnitude (Mw) of 8.2 and an expected peak horizontal ground acceleration at Victoria, 76 kilometres from the epicentre, of 15% of gravity with a 10% probability of occurring in 50 years. At Tofino, which is closer to the locked portion of the subduction zone, the expected peak ground acceleration is 27% of gravity. The lower probability of 2% in 50 years, however, is adopted for the purpose of design and construction. This lower probability carries expected peak ground accelerations of 28% of gravity at Victoria and 52% of gravity at Tofino.

than 1 cycle per second displacing the ground by the same amount, accelerate at only 4% of gravity but can create much damage to high-rise buildings. In cases of very large earthquakes, accelerations close to the epicentre can be more than 80% of gravity, with displacements of many metres. At very distant seismograph stations, however, the ground displacement is barely noticeable and the acceleration almost zero.

Earthquakes
in Diverse Places
Great earthquakes of
the 20th century

For nation shall rise against nation, and kingdom against kingdom:
and there shall be famines, and pestilences, and earthquakes in
diverse places.

— Gospel According to St. Matthew (24:7)

LARGE EARTHQUAKES ARE ONE of nature's most destructive forces. They occur often enough that most people are aware of them, even though few of us have experienced one first hand. Only people living in remote, primitive settings where there are few earthquakes, such as the nomadic Inuit, the Yanomamo of the Amazon, and the Bantu of Africa, have no awareness of these cataclysmic events. People who live outside earthquake zones have a very limited understanding of large earthquakes, generally restricted to media accounts of where they happened and how many people lost their lives. This knowledge doesn't last long because it lacks usefulness. An anonymous quote comes to mind: "It is strange how an earthquake 4000 miles away seems less of a catastrophe than the first scratch on your new car." However, large earthquakes are branded into the memories of people living along the coasts of the Pacific, where such earthquakes are common. This knowledge is useful because it reminds them that earthquakes will happen again.

In this chapter we describe five great earthquakes that have occurred along subduction zones around the Pacific Ocean. Each of the five events gives its own special insights into the likely effects of

The giant Sumatra earthquake of December 2004

The Indonesian earthquake of December 26, 2004, was the second largest quake of the last 100 years, with a moment magnitude of 9.3. Aftershocks reaching magnitude 7.2 occurred for months after the main quake, and a magnitude 8.7 quake ruptured another section of the fault on March 26, 2005. The main earthquake was a subduction zone event similar to quakes that happen off our coast at the Cascadia subduction zone. It occurred along the fault that separates the Australia and Eurasia plates, west and northwest of the island of Sumatra (see map below). There, the Australia plate moves eastward beneath the Eurasia plate along the Sunda Trench west of Thailand and Indonesia. The Eurasia plate includes the Andaman and Nicobar Islands.

The Australia and Eurasia plates had been locked prior to the earthquake of December 26, 2004. Strain had accumulated along the subduction zone for more than 150 years due to convergence of the two plates, and the accumulated strain was released within several tens of seconds by the earthquake. This scenario is believed to be identical to that responsible for great earthquakes at the Cascadia subduction zone in the Pacific Northwest.

The fault separating the Australia and Eurasia plates ruptured over a distance of more than 1200 kilometres. Measurements and computer models indicate that the sea floor slipped up to 5 metres vertically and up to 15 metres horizontally along the fault. Parts of the Andaman and Nicobar Islands were elevated by these movements, whereas land along the western coast of Sumatra subsided up to 2 metres, submerging parts of the coastline.

The catastrophe in the Indian Ocean carries a strong message for residents of the Pacific Northwest. It was a rare event, something that no one in the region had experienced or could imagine. As a result, people, governments, and even scientists were complacent and could not conceive that such an event could happen; they were thus completely unprepared. Scientists in the Pacific Northwest have shown that an earthquake and tsunami nearly identical to that in the Indian Ocean will occur off our coast sometime in the future, although they cannot say when. We are arguably better prepared than people and governments in South Asia were before December 26, 2004, but how will we cope when it is our turn?

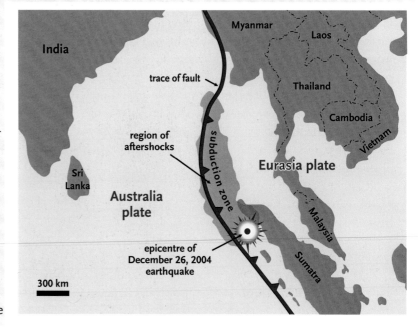

a future great earthquake along the Cascadia subduction zone. The 1964 Alaska earthquake, the strongest ever recorded in North America, is the best analog for a giant earthquake at the Cascadia subduction zone. The 1985 earthquake off the west coast of Mexico shows what can happen to tall buildings constructed on loose sediment far from the epicentre. The 1960 Chile earthquake triggered a devastating tsunami similar to one that occurred in Cascadia in AD 1700. Lastly, great earthquakes in 1944 and 1946 at the Nankai subduction zone east of Japan may be responsible for a series of moderate to large crustal earthquakes that have continued until recently. We use this example to speculate on the possibility that a great Cascadia subduction zone earthquake could trigger later damaging earthquakes on upper crustal faults in the Pacific Northwest.

The Good Friday earthquake in Alaska in 1964 (M_w 9.2) uplifted an 800-kilometre length of the sea floor as much as nine metres and produced a broad neighbouring area of subsidence. This earthquake is the strongest recorded seismic event in North America and the third largest ever recorded.

The Alaska earthquake of 1964

At 5:36 PM on March 27, 1964, a huge earthquake occurred along the coast of southern Alaska at the northeastern end of the Aleutian Trench subduction zone. The initial estimate of surface wave magnitude (M_s, 8.3) greatly under-estimated the strength of the earthquake. A moment magnitude (M_w) of 9.2 was

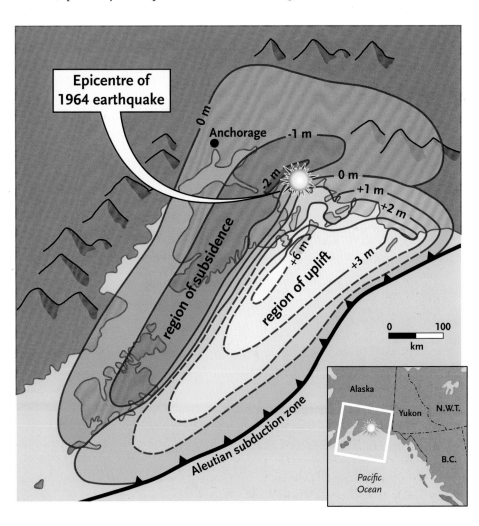

later established when scientists found that an 800-kilometre section of the fault bounding the Pacific and North America plates ruptured during the quake. The earthquake is the third largest seismic event ever recorded. Only the 1960 Chile earthquake (M_w 9.5) and the 2004 Sumatra earthquake (M_w 9.3) were larger. The focal depth could only be roughly estimated at 20 to 50 kilometres due to a lack of nearby seismographs at the time. The closest seismograph was at College, Alaska, more than 430 kilometres from the epicentre. The Mercalli intensity at Anchorage, 160 kilometres from the epicentre, was between VII and IX. The earthquake was felt over an area of 1,800,000 square kilometres, an area nearly twice the size of British Columbia, and there was serious damage over an area of about 200,000 square kilometres. One hundred and fifteen people died in Alaska from the ground shaking and attendant **landslides** and **tsunamis**. An atmospheric shock-wave was recorded in La Jolla, California, 3200 kilometres away, and long-period surface waves raised and lowered most of the North America continent by up to 5 centimetres. **Seiches** were observed in lakes, bays, and inlets throughout North America, particularly in the region bordering the Gulf of Mexico.

The earthquake occurred when the theory of plate tectonics was in its infancy. George Plafker of the United States Geological Survey argued that the source of the earthquake was a fault dipping gently to the north, but at the time the significance of the fault was not known. Scientists knew of the northerly inclined **Wadati-Benioff zone** of earthquakes along the Aleutian Arc, but it was not until submarine trenches were recognized to be subduction zones that a cause for the earthquake became evident. The Wadati-Benioff earthquakes occur within the descending Pacific plate and are mainly due to extensional forces. In contrast, the 1964 quake resulted from compressional forces, as indicated by sudden uplift of a substantial area of the ocean floor parallel to the Aleutian Trench. Unbeknownst to earth

George Plafker (U.S. Geological Survey, retired).

scientists of the day, the plate-boundary thrust fault along the Aleutian Trench had been locked for about 800 years. It suddenly became unstuck on Good Friday, 1964.

This type of earthquake, like the one expected at the Cascadia subduction zone, is called a "subduction thrust earthquake" or, more colloquially, a "megathrust quake." During a subduction thrust earthquake, the overriding plate, in this case North America, is thrust upward and over the subducting oceanic plate. The movement creates a long, narrow band of uplift along the trench. Landward from this zone is a broader region of subsidence. During the Alaska earthquake, a region some 800 kilometres long and about 200 kilometres wide was uplifted by as much as nine metres (see diagram, page 51). The axis of the uplift extended through Middleton Island and south of Kodiak Island. The neighbouring area of subsidence to the northeast was even more extensive. Along its axis, Kenai Peninsula subsided about 2.5 metres, and coastal areas flooded. In Anchorage, the subsidence was about half a metre.

George Plafker and his colleagues drew comparisons between the Aleutian subduction zone and the southern part of the Cascadia subduction zone, for the two share many geological similarities. They concluded that part of the uplift in Alaska was caused by movements along steep, subsidiary, or splay, faults above the main subduction fault. Similar structures exist near the southern end of the Cascadia subduction zone where steep subsidiary thrust faults extend across the seafloor and into northern California. Such faults also occur on the continental

Acoustic image of the sea floor west of Vancouver Island. The interpreted seismic reflection cross-section (annotated face of block diagram) shows faults disrupting sediments that have accumulated at the west edge of the North America plate.

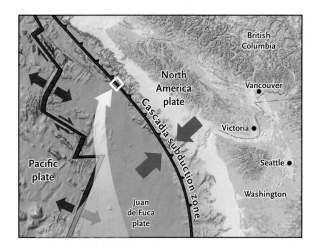

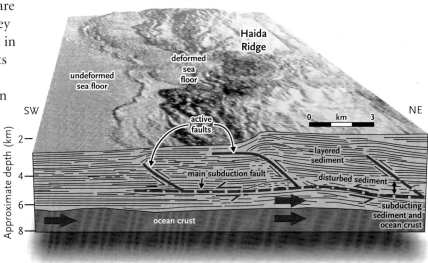

slope off Vancouver Island and are expected to behave in a similar fashion during the next **subduction earthquake**.

Uplift during the earthquake generated tsunamis, and ground shaking caused landslides and **liquefaction**. These three phenomena were responsible for most of the damage to communities in Alaska. The entire economic foundation of Seward on the south coast of Kenai Peninsula was destroyed, and twelve people were killed when a landslide triggered by the earthquake carried the town's waterfront facilities into Resurrection Bay. Ground shaking at Valdez on the northeast side of Prince William Sound caused the **delta** on which the town was built to liquefy. Most of the waterfront facilities and part of the town slid into the sea, triggering a local tsunami that destroyed the entire fishing fleet and what was left of shore installations. Thirty-one people in Valdez lost their lives. The waves generated by the landslide reached heights of over 50 metres.

The main tsunami generated by the earthquake seriously damaged the city of Kodiak on Kodiak Island. Twenty-one people died there, and waterfront installations and boats were extensively

A tsunami inundated part of the town of Valdez, Alaska, immediately after the 1964 earthquake. The tsunami was caused by the collapse of a 1200-metre-long and 180-metre-wide slice of sediment at the front of the delta on which Valdez is located. The wave slammed into the waterfront within two to three minutes of the onset of the earthquake and demolished what was left of the waterfront facilities. The tsunami destroyed the fishing fleet and penetrated about two blocks into the town, killing 31 people.

damaged. The second wave of the tsunami was about 10 metres high when it rolled into Kodiak. It lifted 50- to 100-ton boats over the breakwater and carried them up to three blocks into the city. It was fortunate that a tsunami warning was broadcast before the waves struck, otherwise many more people would have been killed.

But residents of Port Alberni and other communities on Vancouver Island had no such warnings, and tsunami damage was extensive. The incoming waves were amplified as they travelled the 56 kilometres up Alberni Inlet near midnight on March 27. The first wave to arrive at Port Alberni was relatively small and flooded only the lower parts of the town, but the second, 97 minutes later, was over 6 metres high and damaged homes and stores up to a kilometre inland. The respite between the first and second waves allowed residents in low-lying areas to evacuate, and so no lives were lost. Tsunami damage was minor in Washington, but several communities along the Oregon coast were damaged, and Crescent City, California, was particularly hard hit. Sixteen people died in Oregon and California, showing that tsunamis can cause damage far from the earthquake epicentre.

The effects of the Alaska earthquake on Anchorage are particularly instructive, as that city was 160 kilometres from the epicentre, comparable to the distances of Victoria, Nanaimo, Vancouver, Seattle, and Portland from the likely source of a great earthquake at the Cascadia subduction zone. At the time of the earthquake, Anchorage had a population of about 94,500. The tallest buildings were about 14 stories, but most structures, apart from houses, averaged about two stories. Businesses, schools, and churches were mainly empty because the earthquake struck in the late afternoon on a holiday.

There were no seismographs in Anchorage at the time of the quake, thus neither the sequence of seismic waves nor the duration of the shaking was recorded. Residents estimated that the strong

Car moved by the tsunami of the 1964 Alaska earthquake in Port Alberni, British Columbia, about 3000 kilometres from the epicentre.

Fourth Avenue in downtown Anchorage after the 1964 Alaska earthquake. Much of the damage seen in this photograph resulted from a landslide triggered by the ground shaking. Two and one-half blocks of shops, bars, and stores settled until their entrances were below street level. Arrows indicate the direction of ground movement.

The Turnagain Heights district of Anchorage, Alaska, showing damage caused by the 1964 earthquake. Note the widespread ground cracks and scarps (dark areas in lower part of photograph) produced by seismically induced landslides.

shaking lasted between 1.5 and 7 minutes, with most accounts giving 3 to 4 minutes. People in tall buildings felt the shaking for much longer than those in low buildings. Short-period, high-frequency waves rapidly diminished away from the epicentre, and it was mainly the longer period waves that reached Anchorage. These long-period waves had most effect on taller buildings, leaving low buildings largely undamaged. The control tower at the Anchorage International Airport, an unoccupied multi-storey apartment block, and several smaller buildings collapsed. Buildings of ten stories or more suffered moderate to severe damage without collapsing. Several buildings of four to nine stories, however, collapsed or were damaged beyond repair.

The difference in damage was due to differences in the natural period, or frequency, of buildings. High buildings resonated with the seismic waves to a greater degree than low structures. Overall, the direct shaking damage to Anchorage was very selective. Few buildings were totally unaffected, but most small buildings and single-family homes sustained only minor damage. Chimneys toppled and some fire-places separated from adjoining exterior walls. Plaster cracked and objects were thrown to the floors of many homes. Church steeples remained standing and graveyard headstones did not topple. One remarkable photograph shows a snowman still standing beside a damaged house.

Government Hill School in Anchorage, damaged by landsliding induced by the 1964 earthquake. The landslide left part of the school on stable ground and dropped the remainder into a wide trough. Arrows show direction of movement.

Landslides caused most of the damage in Anchorage. The high bluffs bordering Cook Inlet and Turnagain Arm failed massively, destroying many homes, schools, and transportation infrastructure. A buried layer of soft marine clay, called the Bootlegger Cove Clay, suffered a drastic loss of strength due to prolonged, strong shaking. Horizontal slip surfaces developed in the middle of the clay unit, allowing overlying earth materials to move laterally and causing the ground to break up into a chaotic jumble of laterally spreading blocks. Destruction of houses and schools in Turnagain Heights was caused by tilting, cracking, and warping of the surface above the moving debris. In some cases, slide blocks remained intact and houses moved many metres without major damage. Robert B. Atwood, editor and publisher of the *Anchorage Daily Times*, wrote this account of the Turnagain Heights slide:

> *I had just started to practice playing the trumpet when the earthquake occurred. In a few short moments it was obvious that this earthquake was no minor one: the chandelier made from a ship's wheel swayed too much. Things were falling that had never fallen before. I headed for the door. At the door I saw walls weaving. On the driveway I turned and watched my house squirm and groan. Tall trees were falling in our yard. I moved to a spot where I thought*

it would be safe, but, as I moved, I saw cracks appear in the earth. Pieces of ground in jigsaw-puzzle shapes moved up and down, tilted at all angles. I tried to move away, but more appeared in every direction. I noticed that my house was moving away from me, fast. As I started to climb the fence to my neighbor's yard, the fence disappeared. Trees were falling in crazy patterns. Deep chasms opened up. Table-top pieces of earth moved upward, standing like toadstools with great overhangs, some were turned at crazy angles. A chasm opened up beneath me. I tumbled down. I was quickly on the verge of being buried. I ducked pieces of trees, fence posts, mailboxes, and other odds and ends. Then my neighbor's house collapsed and slid into the chasm. For a time it threatened to come down on top of me, but the earth was still moving, and the chasm opened up to receive the house. When the earth movement stopped, I climbed to the top of the chasm. I found angular landscape in every direction. I found my neighbor carrying his young daughter. We found his wife atop one of the high mushroom-like promontories. She was standing alone with her auto, marooned. We climbed up and down chasm walls and under dangerous overhanging pieces of frozen ground to safety.

An interesting concluding statement was made by engineers reporting on their Turnagain slide investigations:

If the duration of ground shaking in the Alaska earthquake had been appreciably shorter, or even comparable to that of many other large earthquakes – 1 to 1.5 minutes perhaps – the slide would probably not have developed, and the area could have been cited as a classic case, illustrating the safety, even during major earthquakes, of slopes underlain by clay soils. In light of such possibilities, experiences of slope failures or nonfailures during earthquakes require careful appraisal before they can be translated to other areas and conditions.

Parts of the Victoria, Vancouver, and Seattle-Tacoma regions are underlain by clayey earth materials somewhat similar to those at Anchorage. Most of the sediments, however, are not as sensitive as the Bootlegger Cove Clay and probably would not fail in the same manner during a subduction earthquake.

Anchorage experienced several other kinds of surface displacements, including ground cracks, **sand blows**, damaging **slumps** and **debris slides**, and avalanches. According to eyewitnesses, many ground cracks opened and closed with the rhythm of the seismic waves, causing extensive damage in the downtown area and elsewhere. Cracks commonly formed near contacts between natural and filled ground. Some buildings straddling these contacts sundered when cracks opened, and several highways, roads, and rail lines built on artificial earth fill were likewise severely damaged. Trees whose roots were held fast in the frozen ground were split due to cracking. Fountains of watery mud and sand appeared where frozen ground overlying watery loose sand cracked during the earthquake. At Turnagain Heights, large sand blows formed by agitation and settlement of slump blocks within the landslide. The sand blows coalesced into ridges up to a metre high, two metres wide, and as much as 30 metres long. One sand blow covered an area of almost 300 square metres.

The significance of the Alaska earthquake to the expected event along the Cascadia subduction zone is the enormity of its energy release; it is the most powerful natural shock known to have struck North America. Its magnitude, ground displacement, strength and duration of ground shaking, and resulting tsunami are what can be expected when the Cascadia subduction zone ultimately unlocks. Pacific Northwest communities are partly built on sensitive ground materials that may liquefy, but a greater hazard is the several minutes of ground shaking that will accompany the great quake. As in Alaska, our coastal communities will sustain the greatest damage, mainly due to the tsunami. Tofino, Ucluelet, Port Alberni, Astoria, Seaside, Newport, and other towns on the Pacific coast will be severely damaged, but with a quick response to the tsunami warning, fewer people may be killed.

The Chile earthquake of 1960

Over the last century, Chile has experienced more than a dozen major earthquakes. The Great Valparaiso earthquake (M_s 8.6) in 1906 damaged much of central Chile and was felt from Peru to Buenos Aires. Another great (M_s 8.3) earthquake in 1939 caused damage over an area of 45,000 square kilometres. The world's most powerful recorded earthquake occurred on May 22, 1960 in southern Chile. Its source was along the Peru-Chile trench, where the **Nazca plate** subducts beneath the **South America plate**. The earthquake had a moment magnitude (M_w) of 9.5 and a surface wave magnitude (M_s) estimated at between 8.4 and 8.5. Its focal depth was 33 kilometres. The main shock was preceded on May 21 by a **temblor** of M_s 7.5 and on May 22 by a series of quakes with M_s magnitudes between 6.5 and 7.5. There were over 50 aftershocks with M_s magnitudes between 5 and 7 in the months following the main shock. The first earthquake, on May 21, was centred south of Concepcion. Aftershocks spread along the fault to the south, culminating in the main shock on May 22.

The earthquakes ruptured more than 1300 kilometres of the subduction fault and released ten times more energy than the 1980 eruption of Mount St. Helens. Landslides similar to those that damaged Anchorage during the 1964 Alaska earthquake were widespread in the epicentral area. Some landslides were so large they changed the course of major rivers or dammed

Comparative maps of the subduction zones responsible for the giant 1960 Chile and 1700 Cascadia earthquakes. The lengths of the rupture zones and the magnitudes of the earthquakes are similar.

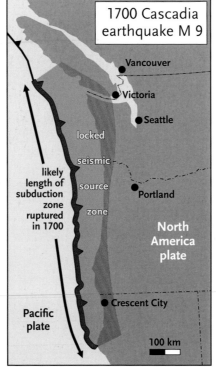

them, creating new lakes. The largest earthquake triggered a devastating tsunami that swept inland up to 25 metres above sea level. Large areas of central coastal Chile subsided suddenly during the earthquake, and some communities and other low-lying areas were submerged beneath up to 2 metres of sea water. The zone of subsidence bordered a zone of uplift to the west, where the sea floor rose up to 6 metres.

The earthquakes left more than 2000 people dead, 3000 injured over 2 million homeless, and caused $4.2 billion damage (2006 dollars). Damage was greatest in the cities of Concepcion, Valdivia, and Puerto Montt. Several small coastal villages were obliterated by the tsunami that came ashore soon after the quake, reaching elevations of up to 25 metres above sea level.

The tsunami was so powerful that it caused 61 deaths in Hawaii, 138 deaths in Japan, and 32 deaths in the Philippines. Total tsunami damage is estimated at over $3.5 billion (2006 dollars). The power of the tsunami is clearly illustrated by its effects in Hawaii and California. The third wave of the tsunami wave train reached Hilo on the big island of Hawaii almost 16 hours after the earthquake. It reached up to 6 metres above sea level, inundating nearly 240 hectares of the town. All of the deaths from the tsunami on the Hawaiian Islands occurred in this area. About 540 businesses and homes in Hilo were destroyed or severely damaged. Destruction was

The coastal fishing village of Queule, Chile, before (top) and after (bottom) the catastrophic earthquake and tsunami of May 1960. Houses, the remains of fishing boats, and uprooted trees were washed as far as two kilometres inland in turbulent surging waters up to 4.5 m deep. The creek in the foreground of the top photograph was changed into an estuary by ground subsidence. The only large tree to survive the tsunami (circled) and the road intersection (white arrows) are common points for both photos.

total in nearly half of the inundated area. Only buildings of reinforced concrete or structural steel, and a few others that were sheltered by these buildings, remained standing, and most of these were gutted. Frame buildings were crushed or floated inland. Dozens of automobiles were wrecked; a 10-ton tractor was swept away; and heavy machinery, mill rollers, and metal stocks were strewn about. Rocks weighing as much as 20 tons were plucked from a sea wall and carried as far as 180 m inland.

The tsunami reached elevations of up to 1.7 metres in California. Two vessels valued at $150,000 (2006 dollars) were lost at Crescent City, California, where the tsunami arrived more than 15 hours after the earthquake. Major damage was reported in Los Angeles and Long Beach harbours. Many thousands of litres of gasoline and oil spilled from overturned boats in these harbours, prompting fears of a fire. At San Diego, ferry service was interrupted after one passenger-laden ferry smashed into a dock, knocking out eight pilings. A second ferry was forced 1.5 km off course and into a flotilla of anchored destroyers.

The 1960 Chile earthquake gave scientists a way to estimate the magnitude of the AD 1700 event at the Cascadia subduction zone. Researchers Kenji Satake, Brian Atwater, and Kelin Wang compared the run-ups of the 1960 Chilean and 1700 Cascadia tsunamis at several sites in Japan. The comparison allowed them to estimate the moment magnitude of the 1700 earthquake in Cascadia as being between 8.9 and 9.1. By inference, the next Cascadia event could be just as large.

Clockwise from top:
Brian Atwater (U.S. Geological Survey); Kenji Satake (Geological Survey of Japan); Kelin Wang (Geological Survey of Canada).

The Mexico City (Michoacan) earthquake of 1985

Mexico City, one of the world's most populous cities, is built on thick, water-saturated lake sediments, mainly silt and clay. Prior to European conquest, the Aztecs constructed their capital on an island in Lake Texcoco. The Spanish drained the lake to allow the city to grow. Although the epicentre of the magnitude (M_s) 8.1 earthquake in 1985 was over 350 kilometres away, many of Mexico City's downtown buildings, located on the old lake bed, either collapsed or were damaged beyond repair.

The Michoacan earthquake occurred at 7:17 AM on Thursday, September 19, 1985. Its epicentre was off the Pacific coast of Mexico, along the subduction zone separating the oceanic **Cocos plate** from North America. The quake seriously affected an area of about 825,000 square kilometre and was felt by almost 20 million people. It also triggered a tsunami that caused some damage to coastal communities near the epicentre, including Lazaro Cardenas, Zihuatenejo, and Manzanillo. Maximum wave heights were about 3 metres at Zihuatenejo and 2.8 metres at Lazaro Cardenas. Seiches were observed in East Galveston Bay, Texas, and in swimming pools in Texas, New Mexico, Colorado, and Idaho.

The epicentre of the 1985 Michoacan earthquake, where the Cocos plate subducts beneath Mexico, was over 350 kilometres from Mexico City. The long-period waves that reached the city caused major damage to many buildings built on soft lake sediments.

Mexico City

little damage to buildings

heavily damaged or collapsed buildings

heavy damage to adobe buildings

Mexico City airport

former lake bed

rock and sediment

lake sediment

1985 earthquake epicentre

Gulf of Mexico

Mexico City

Pacific plate

subduction zone

Cocos plate

500 km

Long-period waves generated by the earthquake reached Mexico City before businesses and schools opened. Even so, 8000 people were killed and 30,000 injured. Over 50,000 people were left homeless. Five hundred buildings were severely damaged or destroyed, contributing to the quake's estimated $7 billion damage (2006 dollars).

The earthquake waves had horizontal ground accelerations of only about 4% of gravity in areas of rock and firm sediment. As a result, higher districts of the city suffered little damage. But surface waves with a 2 to 3 second period were preferentially amplified by resonance in the soft lake sediments in the downtown area. The

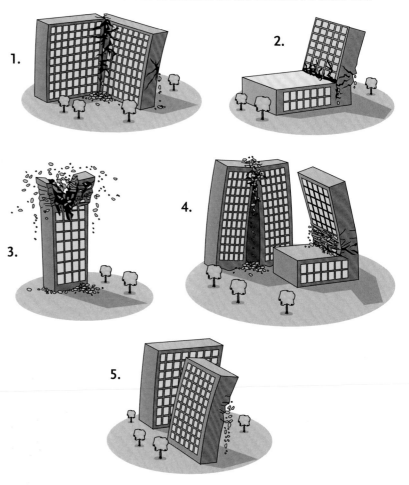

Types of earthquake damage to tall buildings include: (1) breakage of connecting points between buildings that are at right angles to one another and that respond differently to shaking; (2) damage to connecting buildings of different heights with different resonant frequencies; (3) damage to the upper floors of buildings caused by amplification of shaking as seismic waves move upward through the structures; (4) damage due to pounding of adjacent buildings against one another; and (5) damage caused by enhanced swaying of buildings aligned at high angles to the direction of incoming waves.

sediments began to vibrate at their natural period, which is close to that of the long-period seismic waves. The result, as recorded by strong-motion seismographs, was an increase, or amplification, of horizontal accelerations by ten times, to about 40% of gravity. The problem was compounded by the natural vibration properties of buildings that were between 8 and 18 stories high. Those buildings have natural vibration periods of 1 to 2 seconds. They resonated with the seismic waves, swinging back and forth like inverted pendulums. Some swayed so much that they hit one another. Many of the buildings tore themselves apart and collapsed. Buildings less than ten stories high were not severely damaged because their natural resonance periods are shorter than those of the seismic waves. The tallest buildings in the city are 35 stories high and have natural periods of over 3.5 seconds, greater than those of the seismic waves. They too were undamaged.

A lesson learned from the Mexico City earthquake is the relation between the period of seismic waves and the hazard they pose to buildings. Victoria and Nanaimo have few buildings whose natural periods would cause resonance during great earthquakes, but parts of Vancouver, Seattle, and Portland contain high buildings whose

Collapsed and severely damaged multi-storey buildings in Mexico City after the 1985 earthquake. Top: Hotel Continental. Middle: Juarez Hospital, where 400 medical personnel and patients were trapped in the maternity wing. Bottom: collapsed 21-storey steel-frame office building in foreground. The destruction resulted from amplification of seismic waves by lake sediments underlying the city.

natural periods could resonate with long-period waves, producing high horizontal accelerations. In addition, many buildings are located on thick soft sediments that might significantly amplify the seismic waves and thereby the degree of shaking.

The Nankai earthquakes of 1944 and 1946

The Nankai subduction zone is adjacent to the Japanese islands of southwestern Honshu, Shikoku, and Kyushu and is one of the most active earthquake regions on Earth. Great earthquakes occur at this subduction zone, on average, once every 110 years, and seismologists have predicted that a magnitude 8 quake will almost certainly occur there in the next 50 years. The **Philippine Sea plate** converges upon and descends beneath the eastern **Eurasia plate** at the Nankai Trough. In December 1944 and December 1946, two earthquakes with magnitudes (M_s) magnitudes of 8.0 and 8.2, respectively, occurred at Tonankai and Nankaido, situated less than 90 kilometres apart. Each event produced a large tsunami. The 1944 tsunami killed about 900 people. The 1946 tsunami, which was 4 to 7 metres high along the coast and had a maximum run-up of 11 metres above sea level, claimed another 1400 lives. These numbers pale in comparison to the 40,000 people who were killed in the fifteenth century during another great earthquake at the same subduction zone. The three earthquakes ruptured different segments of the same thrust fault that defines the plate boundary along the Nankai Trough.

A significant aspect of the Nankai situation that is relevant to the Cascadia subduction zone is that both illustrate long-term compression parallel to the edge of the continent but continuing short-term contraction in the direction of plate convergence, or perpendicular to the edge of the continent. On page 101, we describe how Vancouver Island appears to be acting as a buttress against the northward-moving Cascades, the result being that small to moderate earthquakes within the North America plate show compression towards the north or northeast, perpendicular to the edge of the buttress. Although the relations between coast-parallel compression and coast-normal contraction at subduction zones are complex, the critical observation at Nankai is that, for at least fifteen years prior to the 1944 earthquake, no earthquakes greater than magnitude 4 occurred in the overriding continental plate. After 1946, however, the number of upper crust earthquakes increased substantially, with some greater than magnitude 6. The devastating Kobe earthquake in 1995 occurred along a fault oriented at an oblique angle to the coast-parallel stress direction. Scientists have recently argued that the Kobe quake was a consequence of the Nankai earthquakes in the 1940s.

These observations imply that, following a future Cascadia subduction earthquake, when coast-normal stress is temporarily reduced, the difference between the coast-parallel and coast-normal stresses could be large enough to activate some pre-existing faults

Comparison of the Nankai subduction zone in Japan and the Cascadia subduction zone in the Pacific Northwest. Moderate to large crustal earthquakes began to occur in Japan after subduction zone earthquakes in 1944 and 1946. The 1944 and 1946 quakes released stresses that had accumulated perpendicular to the coast (long, thin arrows on diagram at the left). The smaller crustal earthquakes, which included the destructive event at Kobe in 1995, resulted from compression parallel to the coast (short, fat red arrows). Similarly, release of stress (shown by the thin red arrows on the diagram at the right) during the next great subduction event in the Pacific Northwest may cause later crustal earthquakes along faults that are being compressed in a north-south direction (fat red arrows).

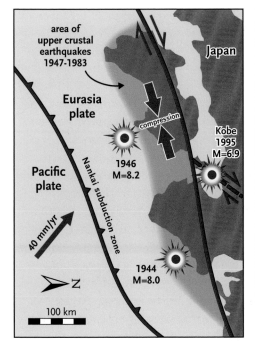

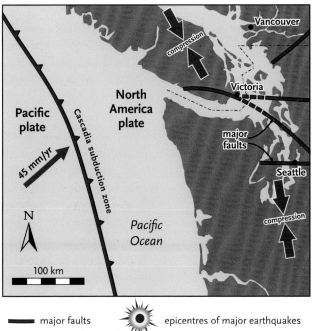

— major faults   epicentres of major earthquakes

within the upper, continental plate. Faults such as the Leech River, South Whidbey Island, and Devils Mountain faults of southern Vancouver Island and northern Puget Lowland are likely candidates, mainly because they are oblique to the coast-parallel stress direction that is the ideal orientation for thrust and strike-slip fault motion. These faults and the Seattle and Portland Hills faults pass through densely populated urban areas. Geologists have found evidence for recent movement on the South Whidbey Island, Devils Mountain, Seattle, and Portland Hills faults (see pages 101 to 108). Similarly, archaeological evidence at Esquimalt Lagoon in Victoria suggests that the Leech River fault may have been active about 2000 years ago. If a Cascadia megathrust earthquake were to trigger a large earthquake on any of these faults, the destruction would be considerable.

Cascadia's Next "Big One"
Geophysical evidence for great earthquakes

Come in consumption's ghastly form,
The earthquake shock, the ocean storm...
— Fitz-Green Halleck, *Marco Bozzaris* (1825)

THE WORD "CASCADIA" is synonymous with the Pacific Northwest. It is a recent socio-economic term embodying similarities in culture, economic aspirations, and even political attitudes of people living in northern California, western Oregon, western Washington, and southwestern British Columbia. It takes its name from the Cascade Range, which include many active and dormant volcanoes, from Lassen Peak in northern California to Mount Meager in southern British Columbia. These volcanoes are the most obvious and dramatic expression of the Cascadia subduction zone.

Fitz-Green Halleck, quoted above, was for many years John Jacob Astor's personal secretary. Halleck's poem has a certain ironic prescience, for Astoria, John Astor's namesake city, may be heavily damaged when the next megathrust earthquake rumbles through Cascadia.

A subduction zone we can call our own

The Cascadia subduction zone forms the boundary between the eastward-moving Juan de Fuca plate and the westward-moving North America plate over a distance of more than 1000 kilometres

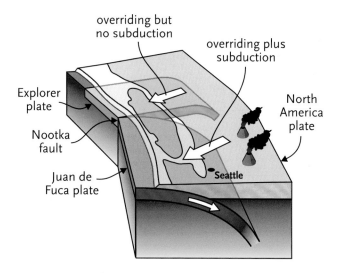

overriding but
no subduction

overriding plus
subduction

Explorer
plate

Nootka
fault

North
America
plate

Juan de
Fuca plate

Seattle

Geometry of plates at the north end of the Cascadia subduction zone. The Nootka fault forms the boundary between the Juan de Fuca plate and the smaller Explorer plate. The Juan de Fuca plate is subducting beneath North America as a single intact crustal block, whereas the Explorer plate is slowly fragmenting as it tries to move beneath North America.

from central Vancouver Island to northern California (pages 15 and 24). At its southern end, the subduction zone is terminated by the Mendocino fracture zone, the offshore continuation of the San Andreas fault, which separates the Pacific and North America plates. In the north, the subduction zone ends at the Nootka fault, which separates the Juan de Fuca plate from the slowly subducting Explorer plate.

Unlike other Pacific subduction zones, no physiographic trench marks the zone of convergence, largely because up to 3 kilometres of sediment cover the eastern edge of the Juan de Fuca plate and because the angle at which this plate subducts beneath the edge of the continent is only two to three degrees, which is very low for subduction zones. The Juan de Fuca plate is only about 9 million years old where it begins to descend beneath the continent off Vancouver Island. Because the plate is young, it is still very hot and therefore buoyant, thus it presses upward against the underside of the overriding continent. This upward force causes the sediment cover on the oceanic plate to be slowly scraped off by the bulldozing action of the westward-moving continent. The scraped-off sediment is added to the continent along a series of faults (see facing page).

An important by-product of this process is the accumulation of methane, generated by decaying organic matter, within the folded and faulted sediments at the base of the continental slope. The methane is driven out of the sediments and slowly rises upward until it freezes below the sea floor to form a layer of frozen **gas hydrate**. Vast quantities of this hydrocarbon have accumulated above subduction zones around the Pacific Ocean and represent the largest natural gas reservoirs in the world. The frozen gas hydrate will remain stable as long as the temperature and pressure are constant. If the seafloor temperature should rise, some of the frozen methane might sublimate and escape into the atmosphere, causing greenhouse warming.

The inclination of the subducting plate increases to about eleven degrees beneath the Pacific coast. Water is driven from the plate at a depth of 100 to 200 kilometres, causing the upper mantle to partially melt. The magma rises upward through the continental crust to the surface, where it erupts at the volcanoes of the Cascade volcanic arc. Measurements of heat flowing from the Earth across Vancouver Island, the Cascade Range, and the continental interior strongly support this scenario. The amount of heat generated within the Earth and reaching the surface decreases across the Juan de Fuca plate and Cascadia subduction zone but dramatically increases over the Cascades and Coast Mountains (diagram, next page).

No earthquakes have been recorded along the interface between the subducting Juan de Fuca plate and the overlying continental crust, even though geophysical and geological data suggest that large subduction earthquakes have occurred in the past and will

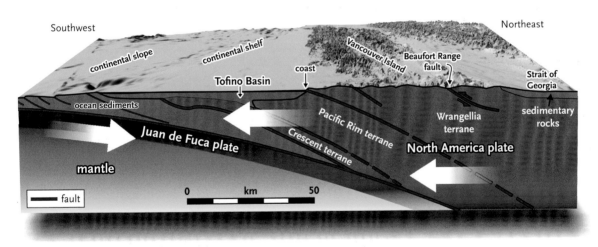

Cross-section through the Earth's crust at the latitude of Barkley Sound on Vancouver Island, showing the structure of the margin of the North American continent. The **Pacific Rim** and **Crescent terranes** underlie **Wrangellia** and are overlain by sedimentary strata of the Tofino Basin. Sediments overlying the subducting Juan de Fuca plate are being scraped off oceanic crust and accreted to the overriding North America plate. Line of cross-section is roughly the same as that on page 98.

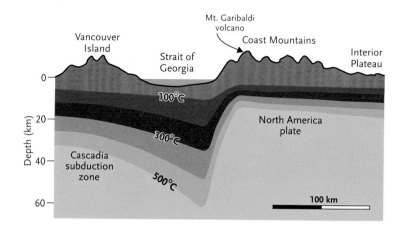

Profile of temperatures through the upper part of the Earth from Vancouver Island eastward to the southern British Columbia interior. The rate of increase of temperature with depth is much lower beneath the Strait of Georgia than beneath the southern Coast Mountains, which are at the north end of the Cascade volcanic chain. The vertical scale is exaggerated.

probably happen again. The last one, on January 26, 1700, is known from geological data and from historical accounts of its tsunami in Japan. The lack of recorded earthquakes at the plate boundary led some scientists to argue in the 1960s and 1970s that great plate-boundary earthquakes do not occur in the Pacific Northwest. A few scientists insisted that subduction was not occurring at all, whereas others argued that subduction was happening, but "quietly," with the oceanic plate slipping silently, or **aseismically**, beneath the continent. Most scientists agreed that the oceanic plate was converging on the continent, as shown by the presence of linear, sea-floor magnetic anomalies beneath the eastern North Pacific Ocean (see page 30). Convergence requires that the oceanic plate be subducting, at least on time scales of thousands of years and more. A scientific breakthrough in the debate came when Tom Heaton of the U.S. Geological Survey and Garry Rogers of the Geological Survey of Canada independently suggested that subduction was not continuous. Rather, on time scales of hundreds of years, the plates are stuck or locked together along part of their boundary and periodically unlock to produce giant earthquakes along the subduction fault.

The approach of the next great earthquake – cocking the gun!

If the two plates are now locked, as suggested by Heaton and Rogers, they must be deforming and we should be able to detect that deformation at the Earth's surface along the subduction zone. For many years, starting before Tom and Garry published their ideas, geophysicists with the U.S. Geological Survey and the Geological Survey of Canada, including Herb Dragert, Mike Schmidt, Jim Savage, and Mike Lisowski, measured small changes in the positions of precisely located geodetic markers on Vancouver Island and the Olympic Peninsula. In addition, ultra-precise measurements of the Earth's gravitational field, which is closely linked to elevation, were repeated at some survey points. Tide gauge records collected over several decades also provided information on small changes in land level on the coast.

Herb Dragert (top), Mike Schmidt (centre) and Roy Hyndman (bottom).

Taken together, the data showed that points on Vancouver Island and Olympic Peninsula were moving eastward and northeastward and rising at a rate of up to several millimetres per year. This may not sound like much, but imagine the energy involved in deforming such vast tracts of the Earth's crust by even such small amounts. Also, bear in mind that the process is ongoing – after 100 years, the changes would amount to many tens of centimetres. Even more precise measurements, with accuracies of a few millimetres, are now possible with satellite global positioning systems (GPS). Measurements of precisely located survey points at Victoria and at Penticton in the continental interior have demonstrated that the two sites are moving closer together at an average rate of about 7 millimetres per year.

This surface deformation pattern is consistent with a

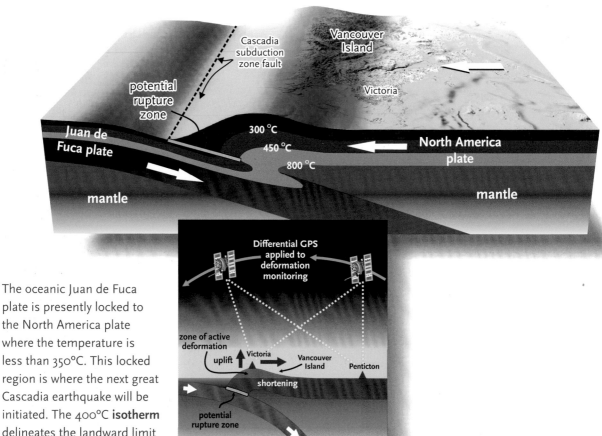

The oceanic Juan de Fuca plate is presently locked to the North America plate where the temperature is less than 350°C. This locked region is where the next great Cascadia earthquake will be initiated. The 400°C **isotherm** delineates the landward limit of potential rupture. Vancouver Island is being flexed upward due to compression and elastic shortening of the North America plate above the locked interface. This deformation has been detected from satellite measurements of small changes in the relative position of points on the Earth's surface. Some time within the next several hundred years the plates will suddenly unlock, triggering a great earthquake.

locked fault along the subduction zone. The western margin of North America is being squeezed above the locked part of the megathrust fault due to convergence of the North America and Juan de Fuca plates. This spells trouble – we live in an area that is accumulating huge amounts of energy that will someday be released in a giant earthquake when the fault ruptures. Canadian geophysicists Roy Hyndman and Kelin Wang have estimated the probable size of this earthquake by determining the extent of the locked portion of the plate boundary (diagram, facing page). The extent of the locked zone is important, because earthquake magnitude is linked to the area of fault rupture. Its location is equally important, because that will partly determine the intensity of ground shaking in our communities. Roy and Kelin delineated the locked zone from the pattern and extent of surface deformation and from estimates of temperatures at various positions along the megathrust fault. A critical assumption in their work is that the deformation is elastic, that is, energy stored in the crust will be completely released during the earthquake. Such an analysis is not without uncertainties, and other earth scientists have used other types of information to map the locked zone. The results differ in detail, but most scientists agree that a portion of the megathrust fault averaging several tens of kilometres wide and perhaps 1000 kilometres long is locked.

If the entire locked zone were to rupture at once, the resulting earthquake would have a magnitude of at least 9, like the last quake in AD 1700. In contrast, a rupture of a segment of the locked zone, say 100 to 200 kilometres long, as others have suggested, would produce a magnitude 8 quake. Rupture of one segment, however, could potentially trigger rupture of adjacent segments some days, years, or even decades later as happened at the Nankai subduction zone of Japan in 1944 and 1946. In such a case, the "big one" becomes two or more, closely spaced, somewhat smaller "big ones." As described on pages 66 and 67, comparisons between the stress regime of the Cascadia subduction zone and that of the Nankai subduction zone suggest that a great subduction earthquake might trigger rupture along a crustal fault up to several decades later, producing a shallow quake of magnitude 7 or larger. If that earthquake were centred close to one of our big cities, for example along the Leech River fault near Victoria, or the Seattle or Portland Hills faults, the damage might be greater than that of a much larger but more distant subduction quake.

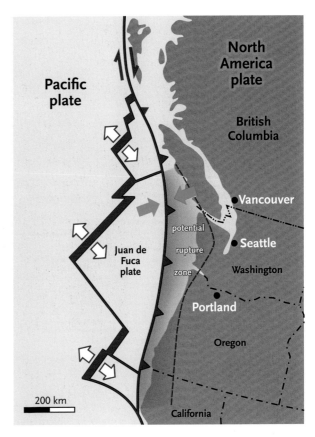

Approximate extent of the locked portion of the fault separating the Juan de Fuca and North America plates. Part of the entire locked zone will rupture during a future great earthquake. Green arrows show the direction of convergence of the Juan de Fuca and North America plates.

75

During the last few years, Canadian geophysicist Herb Dragert and his colleagues in the United States and Japan have made important advances in understanding the accumulation of strain energy across the subduction fault beneath southern Vancouver Island. Using data from continuously monitoring GPS stations, they recognized episodes of slip along the megathrust fault at depths of 20 to 40 kilometres, well landward of and below the locked portion of the fault. Simultaneously, Garry Rogers identified non-earthquake tremors at about the same depth, and at the same time, as the slip events. One might think that these slip events would relieve strain across the fault. But in fact the opposite is true, because strain increases up-dip along the locked part of the fault during each episode of slip on the deeper, unlocked part. In effect, the silent slip events ratchet up the strain on the locked portion of the fault. The slip events occur at intervals of 13 to 15 months, last from 10 to 20 days, and migrate laterally along the length of the subduction zone. It is conceivable that a future "silent slip" event will trigger a giant megathrust earthquake and that its associated tremors indicate times of increased probability of such an event. The trick will be to recognize the specific slip event that "breaks the

Slow-slip events along the deep portion of the Cascadia subduction zone and non-earthquake tremor activity recorded in the Victoria area. The blue circles represent day-to-day changes in the position of a GPS site at Victoria with respect to a GPS site near the inland city of Penticton, British Columbia, which is assumed to be stationary and fixed to the North America plate. The red line segments show the progressive movements between slip events, marked by reversals every 13 to 16 months. Since 1996 Victoria has moved about 40 millimetres closer to Penticton. The bottom graph shows the number of hours of tremor activity per 10-day period for southern Vancouver Island. Slip events last from 10 to 20 days.

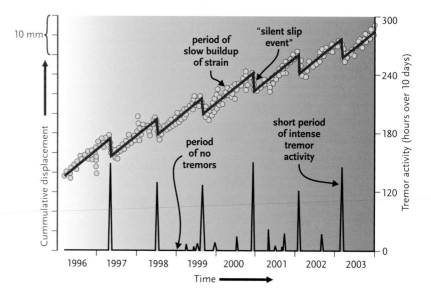

camel's back." If that can someday be done, the tremors might give us a few days to prepare for the big one.

A giant megathrust earthquake could trigger large landslides, up to many kilometres in length beneath the sea, on the continental slope off Oregon, Washington, and Vancouver Island. Several large landslides have been found in acoustic images of the deep sea floor in these areas. Such massive landslides trigger tsunamis or could expose frozen methane hydrate to the ocean, thus releasing large quantities of the gas into the ocean and atmosphere. We may have a better handle on this threat by the end of the decade. In 2003, the governments of Canada and British Columbia approved funding for the Canadian part of the Neptune Project, a $300 million network of connected instruments to be placed on the seafloor off the coasts of southern British Columbia, Washington, and Oregon. Three thousand kilometres of fibre-optic cable will be laid over an ocean floor area of 200,000 square kilometres to provide real-time data on earthquakes and crustal motion to shore stations at the University of Victoria, University of Washington and in Oregon.

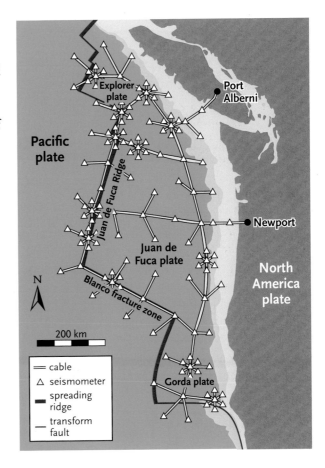

The Neptune Project is a joint Canadian-U.S. scientific initiative to install a variety of scientific recording instruments on the sea floor at the surface of the Juan de Fuca plate. The instruments include seismometers and GPS tracking devices that will continuously monitor seismicity and crustal movements at the Cascadia subduction zone. The instruments will be connected to one another by several thousand kilometres of fibre-optic communication and power cables.

Ghostly stems of conifers in a tidal marsh at Copalis River, Washington; note person for scale. The trees were killed soon after the last great earthquake at the Cascadia subduction zone in AD 1700. They subsided 1 to 2 metres, from a position at the forest edge into the intertidal zone, where they were killed by brackish tidal waters. The roots and lower part of the tree stems are buried beneath tidal mud that has been deposited since the earthquake.

Sleuthing
Past "Big Ones"
Geologic evidence for great earthquakes

With a system as complicated as the earth, almost anything can happen occasionally.

— E.C. Bullard (1966)

W E KNOW FROM OUR BRIEF, 200-year historical record that the coastal Pacific Northwest is earthquake-prone. Our written history, however, extends back only to the early decades of the nineteenth century, and instrumented records of earthquakes are even shorter, spanning only the past hundred years. The first, large, documented earthquake happened in 1872, had an epicentre in north-central Washington, and is estimated to have been larger than magnitude 7. No seismometers recorded the quake, and our knowledge of it is based on sketchy contemporary newspaper accounts. In comparison, the Chinese have written records of earthquakes dating back more than 3000 years, and the Japanese for about 500 years; consequently their understanding of the seismic risk they face is much better than ours. The Pacific Northwest's instrumented earthquake record is too short – it cannot reliably be used to predict the maximum size of events that can occur or to know if large quakes happen in clusters in either time or space. Until very recently, our best risk assessments were based on comparisons with other, geologically similar, earthquake-prone regions such as Alaska, California, Japan, and Chile, all of which have sustained considerable damage during large earthquakes. Of course, as time passes and we experience additional strong earthquakes, all of which will be well recorded by numerous seismographs, our understanding of seismic processes will improve.

In the meantime, is there anything we can do to increase our understanding of local seismic risk? Yes. By using geological data, we can extend the historical record of earthquakes back hundreds, even thousands, of years. This chapter tells how geologists and geophysicists are arriving at a better understanding of the threat. The premise is simple – the land retains traces of large earthquakes that occurred long ago, and this record can be read by people who know the language.

Tell-tale signs from marshes, lakes, and the deep sea

We begin our story in the marshes of Willapa Bay, a large tidal estuary on the coast near the southwest corner of the state of Washington. In the late 1980s, Brian Atwater of the United States Geological Survey (USGS) went there to test Tom Heaton's hypothesis that the lack of earthquakes along the Cascadia megathrust fault was due to locking of the North America and Juan de Fuca plates.

This tidal marsh borders Niawiakum River, which flows into Willapa Bay in southwest Washington. A vertical succession of tidal marsh soils beneath the modern marsh records seven great earthquakes over the past 3500 years. The box indicates the location of the photograph on page 82.

Heaton and Garry Rogers compared the Cascadia subduction zone to other, similar subduction zones around the Pacific, all of which have generated great, magnitude 8 or 9 quakes. They concluded that the accumulating strain energy across the locked subduction fault would, at some time, be released in a giant earthquake. They further argued that the return period for great earthquakes in Cascadia could be several hundred years, longer than the period since the first European contact on this coast. Their hypothesis proved controversial and was criticized by other earth scientists, some of whom argued that the reason for the lack of earthquakes along the subduction fault was that the Juan de Fuca plate was subducting silently, or aseismically.

Brian Atwater decided to try to resolve the issue by searching for telltale geological evidence of the earthquakes. Brian reasoned that, if subduction zones elsewhere around the Pacific are analogous to the Cascadia subduction zone, as Heaton and Rogers argued, prehistoric subduction earthquakes in Cascadia perhaps would produce similar effects to the great 1960 Chile and 1964 Alaska earthquakes. Specifically, a great subduction earthquake in the coastal Pacific Northwest would cause much or all of the Pacific coast bordering the subduction zone to suddenly subside up to two

Series of cartoons showing submergence of a tidal marsh and forest during a great Cascadia earthquake (panel 2), deposition of sand during the tsunami that follows the quake (panel 3), and burial of the submerged tidal flat beneath mud and recolonization by marsh plants (panel 4). The succession of sediments produced by these events is the tell-tale geologic signature of a great earthquake.

1. Coastal forest	2. Great earthquake; land sinks, flooding forest	3. Within an hour tsunami rushes ashore	4. Dead forest in a tidal flat	5. "Ghost" forest

    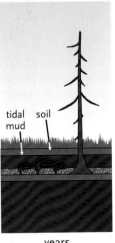

before the earthquake	during the earthquake	tsunami	after the earthquake	years later

Exposure of sediments in the bank of the Niawiakum River in southwest Washington (page 80). The peat layer seen here is abruptly overlain by tsunami sand and tidal mud. The peat represents a former marsh that subsided 1 to 2 metres during the last great subduction earthquake in the Pacific Northwest in AD 1700. The down-dropped marsh was overrun by a tsunami, which deposited the sand. Later, mud gradually settled out of tidal waters onto the sand-blanketed marsh. Divisions on the scale are 1 centimetre.

metres, as happened in both Alaska and Chile (see illustrations on pages 51 and 61). This proved to be a critical inference, because it gave Atwater targets for field work – coastal tidal marshes.

Atwater further reasoned that if a great earthquake were to occur today, Pacific coastal marshes, which lie just above average sea level, would subside and thus be drowned, killing the plants that grow on them. Tidal waters would deposit mud on the drowned marsh plants, eventually entombing them in tens of centimetres of sediment. This sequence of events would, theoretically, produce distinct layers beneath the surface of the marsh – a layer of peat, representing the down-dropped marsh and, abruptly overlying it, a layer of grey mud. Knowing that this couplet would be produced if a great subduction earthquake occurred today, Atwater reasoned that it would also result from such an earthquake in the past. Presumably, any protected tidal marsh on the Pacific coast inland of the subduction zone would show this distinctive **stratigraphy** for each great earthquake recorded in the marsh. Not stopping there, however, Brian was able to focus his investigation even further.

He was aware of "ghost forests" in some tidal marshes bordering Willapa Bay. The ghost forests comprise bleached skeletons of large red cedars surrounded by intertidal marsh plants (page 78). The trees could not have grown in their present brackish-water setting and they had not been killed by fire. Atwater asked, could they have been dropped down into the intertidal zone from a higher elevation during an earthquake? He discovered that the trees were rooted in soil buried beneath a layer of tidal mud about a metre thick, upon which the modern marsh had become established (see photo page 85). He could trace the buried soil both landward to adjacent higher ground and seaward towards Willapa Bay. It appeared that Brian had found the "smoking gun" of the last

tidal
mud

tsunami sand layers

peat

Small plants tell a large story

Fossil plants and animals preserved in sediments that underlie the tidal marshes at Willapa Bay provide support for Brian Atwater's hypothesis that the Pacific coast of Washington dropped up to 2 metres during each of many great earthquakes in the past. In the 1980s, Brian enlisted the help of Eileen Hemphill-Haley, an expert on **diatoms**, which are microscopic algae with siliceous skeletons. Diatoms are common aquatic organisms that live in the sea, fresh and brackish waters, and moist soil. The species differ according to the environments in which they live. In coastal wetlands, for example, different groups of species live in freshwater marshes, tidal marshes, and unvegetated tidal flats. In essence, diatoms are sensitive recorders of elevation, and their fossils provide a record of former wetland elevation when the diatoms were living.

Hemphill-Haley extracted many thousands of diatom skeletons from sediment samples that she collected in vertical sequences of the sediments that Atwater had documented at Willapa Bay. She found that the buried peat layers contain diatoms that tolerate only relatively dry, freshwater conditions present in the highest parts of the Willapa Bay tidal marshes. In contrast, the mud samples collected directly above the peats contain very different diatoms, ones that are found today only in the lower, wetter and more saline part of the tidal zone. By comparing the modern elevation zones of the two assemblages, Hemphill-Haley concluded that the former marshes, represented by the peat layers, had dropped 1 to 2 metres and then been buried at their new, lower elevations by tidal muds. The cause of the recurrent, sudden subsidence was successive great earthquakes at the Cascadia subduction zone.

Eileen Hemphill-Haley.

Diatoms are microscopic, single-celled plants that live in lakes, estuaries, marshes, and the sea. The species of diatoms shown in this photo live in tidal marshes; their distributions are controlled by salinity and duration of flooding by tidal waters.

great earthquake on the coast. Before the quake, the cedars were growing near the edge of the tidal marsh. During the quake, they dropped about 2 metres to a position within the range of tides. The roots of the trees became submerged in brackish water and the trees quickly died. Shortly thereafter, mud accumulated around the roots of the trees, over time building up to a thickness of nearly 1 metre.

One such occurrence does not prove the Heaton and Rogers hypothesis, but Atwater and

Carbon dating

Scientists have developed many tools for dating events that occurred hundreds to billions of years ago. The most widely used method for "young" events (up to about 50,000 years old) is **radiocarbon dating**. This method was developed in the late 1940s by Willard Libby, a physicist working at the University of California. Here's how it works. Carbon occurs in three forms, or **isotopes**, in the atmosphere: ^{12}C, which makes up about 98.89% of atmospheric carbon, ^{13}C (1.11%), and ^{14}C (0.0000000001%). The first two of these isotopes are stable. The third, ^{14}C, is radioactive, thus unstable, and gradually decays to a stable form of nitrogen. The rate of decay of ^{14}C is constant. If you start with 100 atoms of ^{14}C, 50 will decay to nitrogen in 5730 years and 50 will remain. One-half of one-half, or one-quarter, of the atoms (25) will remain after 11,460 (5730 plus 5730) years. The ratio of ^{14}C to ^{12}C in the atmosphere, however, remains approximately constant over time because unstable ^{14}C atoms are continually being produced by cosmic rays that enter the atmosphere from outer space.

What allows scientists to use the decay of ^{14}C to date geologic events is that all organisms, be they plants or animals, incorporate atmospheric carbon in their tissues and hard parts. While a plant or animal is living, the ratio of ^{14}C to ^{12}C remains in equilibrium with that in the atmosphere due to photosynthesis in plants and metabolism in animals. Once the organism dies, however, no more ^{14}C is added to the plant or animal and the carbon "clock" starts to "tick," with ^{14}C gradually decreasing relative to ^{12}C. All one has to do to determine the age of a fossil plant or animal is measure its $^{14}C/^{12}C$ ratio and, from that, determine the amount of time that has elapsed since the clock started ticking. To relate this age to the time of a geological event of interest, the plant or animal must have died at the time of the event. An example, in the case of a great earthquake, would be a marsh plant that was drowned and buried beneath mud shortly after the quake.

other scientists, including one of the authors (JC), soon found the same telltale peat-mud couplet in marshes along the entire 1000-kilometre length of the Cascadia subduction zone, from western Vancouver Island to northern California. **Fossils** within the buried peat layer are typical marsh plants such as sedges (*Carex*), rushes (*Juncus*), and grasses (Gramineae); some are so well preserved they appear to have died yesterday. **Carbon dating** of the plants showed that they died at about the same time as the earthquake, in the late 1600s or early 1700s.

The annual growth rings observed in cores extracted from the ghost cedars have patterns much like commercial bar codes. In the early 1990s, U.S. researcher David Yamaguchi compared the ring patterns of the ghost cedars with those of nearby old living trees. He found matches and determined that the outermost preserved rings in the dead cedars date to the last decade or two of the 1600s, suggesting that the earthquake happened shortly after that time. The bark and true outer rings of the ghost cedars, however, had been weathered away over the past three centuries, and a more precise date for the earthquake would not come for several more years.

The peat layer supporting the ghost cedars was not the only one in the Willapa Bay marshes. Atwater found a vertical sequence of up to seven such layers, each abruptly overlain by tidal mud. He argued that each of the couplet layers records a past great subduction earthquake. Carbon dating of fossil plants in the peat layers provided approximate ages for the events. The results show that the seven earthquakes occurred during the last 3500 years, which gives an average of one quake about every 500 years (see illustration on page 86). However, the earthquakes did not occur, like clockwork, every 500 years. Rather, intervals between two successive quakes range from as little as about 100 years to nearly 1000 years.

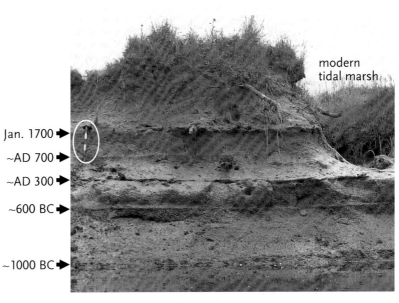

Support for Brian Atwater's conclusions soon came from another source. In the late 1980s, John Adams, a seismologist with the Geological Survey of Canada, studied cores of deep-sea sediments that had been collected off the coasts of Washington and Oregon by Oregon State University scientists. The cores contained a succession of mud layers deposited by **turbidity currents**, dense, bottom-hugging flows of sediment-laden water that move rapidly down **submarine canyons** on the **continental slope** into the deep ocean. The sediments deposited by turbidity currents are called **turbidites** and most commonly result from submarine slope failures.

John showed that the turbidites in the various cores were the products of slope failures that occurred at widely separated localities along the edge of the Washington and Oregon **continental shelf**. More importantly, he was able to correlate the turbidites from one locality to another and show that they are of the same age. In other words, numerous landslides had occurred repeatedly and at the same time over a large length of the continental shelf edge. John inferred that contemporaneous submarine slope failures over such a vast area could only be caused by large earthquakes, and he suggested that

Evidence for five large earthquakes can be seen in this tidal channel at Willapa Bay, Washington. Fossil tidal marsh soils (dark horizons, indicated by arrows) represent old marsh surfaces, each of which subsided 1 to 2 metres during an earthquake. After the earthquakes, the marsh surfaces were buried by tidal mud (light-coloured layers). The dates on the left side of the photograph are approximate ages of the earthquakes. The uppermost buried soil records the last great subduction earthquake in January 1700. During the next subduction earthquake, the modern marsh (top surface) will subside and become covered with sea water. Over time, tidal mud will bury the marsh, providing the substrate for a new marsh. The underlying sediments will record this story. Divisions on shovel handle (circled) are 10 centimetres.

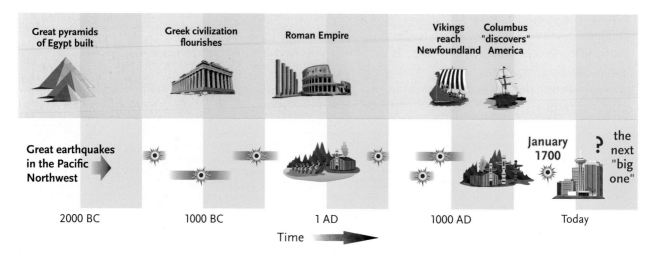

Great pyramids of Egypt built — **Greek civilization flourishes** — **Roman Empire** — **Vikings reach Newfoundland** — **Columbus "discovers" America**

Great earthquakes in the Pacific Northwest

January 1700 — ? the next "big one"

2000 BC — 1000 BC — 1 AD — 1000 AD — Today

Time

Times of the last seven great subduction earthquakes in the Pacific Northwest. Only the last of the seven earthquakes is precisely dated; it occurred on January 26, 1700. The other six quakes have been dated using the radiocarbon technique, which gives only approximate ages. The horizontal bars on the earthquake symbols indicate the intervals in which the earthquakes occurred.

John Adams

the earthquakes were the same subduction events that Brian Atwater had documented. The cores contained a distinctive layer of **volcanic ash** that is about 7400 years old. The ash was deposited shortly after Mount Mazama (now Crater Lake, Oregon) destroyed itself in a cataclysmic eruption, throwing several tens of cubic kilometres of ash and other volcanic debris into the stratosphere. Adams found 13 turbidite layers above the Mazama ash layer in the cores and concluded that large subduction earthquakes have occurred, on average, once every 500 to 600 years, close to the 500-year **recurrence interval** suggested by Atwater. Adams' ideas have recently been tested and extended by a group of other researchers led by Chris Goldfinger of Oregon State University. Goldfinger's team confirmed Adams' conclusions and extended his record of great earthquakes back to 10,000 years ago, documenting 18 events over that period.

Let's return to the last great Cascadia earthquake in the coastal Pacific Northwest. Our knowledge of the 1960 Chile and 1964 Alaska earthquakes tells us that a Cascadia quake would trigger a tsunami as well as liquefaction at several localities where soft, surface silty and sandy sediments are affected by strong ground shaking. Evidence abounds on the Pacific coast for a tsunami about 300 years ago, immediately after the coasts of Vancouver Island, Washington, Oregon, and northern California suddenly subsided up to 2 metres. At many tidal marshes, a layer of sand occurs between the approximately 300-year-old buried marsh peat and the overlying tidal mud. The layer becomes thinner and the sand finer in a landward direction. It pinches out on rising ground bordering the marshes. The sand also contains microscopic marine fossils and, in some cases, shells of intertidal clams and snails, indicating that it has an offshore source. Only a tsunami or storm could deposit such a sand layer. A tsunami is the most likely cause, because sandy sediment is rare in most Pacific Northwest tidal marshes, whereas storms are common and should leave abundant evidence in the marshes if they were the explanation for the sand layers. Further, the sand typically occurs only at one stratigraphic level – directly on top of buried peat layers. If storms had deposited the sand layers, the layers would occur randomly through the sequence, but such is not the case.

Chris Goldfinger

In the 1990s, U.S. and Canadian geologists, including Harvey Kelsey, Alan Nelson, Peter Bobrowsky, Ian Hutchinson, Harry Williams, and one of the authors (JC) cored several low-elevation coastal lakes and found layers of sand that they attributed to tsunamis. The most complete record comes from Bradley Lake in northern Oregon, where Kelsey and co-workers documented fourteen separate tsunami sand layers deposited over the past 7500 years. Carbon dating shows that many of the Bradley Lake sand layers are the same age as subsidence events documented in tidal

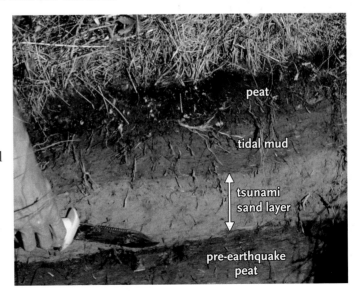

Bed of sand left by a tsunami in January 1700. The sand is exposed in a shallow pit dug into a tidal marsh near Tofino on the west coast of Vancouver Island. It was deposited on a marsh that subsided during the earthquake and was later covered by tidal mud.

peat

tidal mud

tsunami sand layer

pre-earthquake peat

Clockwise from top left: Harvey Kelsey (Humboldt State University), Alan Nelson (U.S. Geological Survey), Ian Hutchinson (Simon Fraser University), and Harry Williams (University of North Texas).

marshes. This is to be expected, because the tsunamis and subsidence events are linked. Some of the layers of tsunami sand in the lakes, however, do not appear to have counterparts in the marshes.

Evidence has also been found for liquefaction, generated by several minutes of strong ground shaking during the last subduction earthquake. The evidence includes veins of sand extending up through tidal marsh peat and mud exposed along the banks of the Columbia River between the Pacific coast and Portland. The veins, which are properly termed **clastic dykes**, record the rapid upward movement of a slurry of sand from a liquefied sand layer at depth. The clastic dykes along the Columbia River are known to be associated with the last subduction earthquake because they rise to the level of the 300-year-old buried marsh. They do not extend higher, as they would if they were younger than the buried marsh. Some of the clastic dykes terminate in large, low mounds many metres across that rest on the buried marsh peat. The mounds are sand blows or **sand volcanoes**, accumulations of liquefied sediment erupted onto the marsh during the earthquake.

Liquefaction of water-saturated silt or sand during an earthquake may cause the ground to fracture and subside, damaging or destroying buildings and other human works.

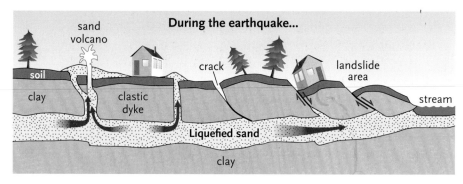

So, there you have it: four lines of evidence (subsidence, submarine landslides, tsunami, and liquefaction), providing strong evidence for recurrent great earthquakes centred within 200 kilometres of all the large cities in the coastal Pacific Northwest. Although these earthquakes clearly have happened in the past, we have not had one since European settlement. Can we be sure that we will experience another of these monsters and, if so, when and how large will it be? The answer to the first question is an unequivocal "Yes." The answer to the second question is that we don't know, but it will certainly happen within the next 500 years. The quake will have a magnitude of at least 8; it might exceed magnitude 9.

Historical evidence

Carbon dating and Japanese writings tell us that the last great subduction earthquake in the Pacific Northwest occurred nearly a century before the explorations of the coast by Captain James Cook in 1778. That the earthquake had a profound impact on aboriginal people living on the coast is shown by their oral traditions of the event. The traditions speak of strong ground shaking and a devastating tsunami on a cold winter night when widespread damage was done to settlements along the Pacific coast from Vancouver Island to northern California. For example, the following account comes from the Nuu-Chah-nulth people at Pachena Bay, on the west coast of Vancouver Island:

> *This story is about the first !Anagl'a or "Pachena Bay" people. It is said they were a big band at the time of him whose name was Hayoqwis'is, "Ten-On-Head-On-Beach." He was the Chief, he was one of the Pachena Bay tribe, he owned the Pachena Bay country. Their village site was Loht'a; they of Loht'a live there. I think they numbered over a hundred persons... There is no one left alive due to what this land does at times. They had no way or time to try to save themselves. I think it was at nighttime that the land shook... They were at Loht'a, and they simply had no*

3 hours after earthquake

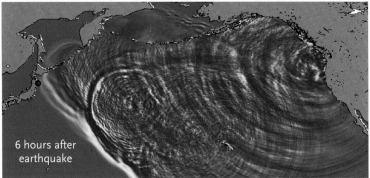

6 hours after earthquake

time to get hold of canoes, no time to get awake. They sank at once, were all drowned; not one survived … I think a big wave smashed into the beach. The Pachena Bay people were lost … But they on their part who lived at Mal:ts'a:s, "House-Up-Against-Hill", the wave did not reach because they were on high ground. Right against a cliff were the houses on high ground at M'a:lsit, "Cold-Water-Pool." Because of that they came out alive. They did not drift out to sea along with the others. [Quoted from E.Y. Arima and others, 1991, Canadian Museum of Civilization, Canadian Ethnology Series, Mercury Series Paper 121.]

Computer-simulation of the tsunami generated by the AD 1700 earthquake at the Cascadia subduction zone. The earthquake ruptured the entire 1000-kilometre length of the boundary between the North America and Juan de Fuca plates off the coasts of Vancouver Island, Washington, Oregon, and northern California. This simulation shows the progress of the tsunami across the Pacific Ocean three and six hours after the earthquake. The orange and yellow colours correspond to the crests of waves. The tsunami has been precisely dated from written records from Kuwagaski (red circle) in Japan. The earthquake that caused it occurred at about 9 PM Pacific Standard Time on January 26, 1700.

Another story from the Cowichan Valley on Vancouver Island says that "in the days before the white man there was a great earthquake. It began about the middle of one night … threw down houses and brought great masses of rock down from the mountains. One village was completely buried beneath a landslide."

The tsunami was also recorded in Japan, where it caused considerable damage to communities on the east coast of Honshu (see pages 91 to 93). The Japanese records are the basis for dating the earthquake to the night of January 26, 1700, presumably the "cold winter night" mentioned in the native oral traditions. In addition, comparison of inferred wave run-ups of the 1700 Cascadia tsunami with recorded run-ups of the 1960 Chile and 1964 Alaska tsunamis at the same sites in Japan supports the estimate of magnitude 9 for the 1700 earthquake.

The great AD 1700 earthquake

It is called a "ghost forest," the stand of white skeletons of dead cedars in a tidal marsh at the shores of Willapa Bay on the southwest coast of Washington (page 78). Someone seeing this ghostly forest might ask, "How could trees have grown in a tidal marsh and what killed them?" The answers to these questions were provided by geologist Brian Atwater in the late 1980s. Brian showed that the trees were not rooted in the modern marsh, but rather in an old marsh buried by over a metre of tidal mud. He mapped out the buried surface, which he found to be marked by a thin layer of peat, and showed that it extends throughout the modern marsh. He and his American and Canadian co-workers found the same peat layer in over 20 tidal marshes extending from central Vancouver Island to northern California. Carbon dating showed that the peat layer at all of the sites is about 300 years old, although exact age equivalence could not be proved because the dating technique is too imprecise.

Atwater proposed that the peat layer was an old marsh that subsided during a great earthquake about 300 years ago. Cedars growing at the edge of the marsh also subsided and were killed by brackish tidal waters that inundated their roots. The presence of the same soil over a 1000-kilometre length of the Pacific coast supports the argument that the earthquake was very large. Based on comparisons with earthquakes in Chile in 1960 and Alaska in 1964, scientists suggested that the 1700 quake may have had a moment magnitude of 9 or more.

In the 1990s, scientists asked themselves "How can we date this event more precisely?" American and Japanese researchers independently tried two approaches. The Americans looked at the pattern of annual rings in trees killed or damaged by the earthquake and matched them to ring patterns of living trees many hundreds of years old that had not been affected by the quake. Most

of the stems of standing earthquake-killed trees are weathered, thus the exact year of death of the trees cannot be determined. However, researchers eventually precisely dated the outermost ring of well preserved roots of some of these trees to AD 1699. This "kill" date matches perfectly the year of the annual ring marking injury to several trees that survived the earthquake.

The Japanese researchers were even cleverer. They read in one of Brian Atwater's papers that he had found an anomalous layer of sand resting on the buried peat layer at Willapa Bay and had suggested that the sand had been deposited by a tsunami triggered by the earthquake that had caused the killing of the coastal marshes. The Japanese, led by Kenji Satake, being very familiar with tsunamis, hypothesized that a large tsunami generated near the west coast of North America would cross the Pacific Ocean and strike Japan. The researchers searched Japanese written records and discovered that a mysterious tsunami, which had not been accompanied by a local earthquake, occurred on January 27, 1700. The tsunami struck a 1000-kilometre length of the eastern coast of Honshu with waves up to several metres high, causing considerable damage in some towns. The researchers concluded that the tsunami was triggered by the same earthquake that had caused the land to drop on the west coast of North America and killed the cedars shortly after 1699. They did even better – they back-calculated the travel time of the tsunami to Japan (some nine hours), factored in the change in time zones, and concluded that the earthquake occurred at about 9 PM Pacific Standard Time on January 26, 1700! Moreover, the Japanese scientists made an estimate of the magnitude of the earthquake based on wave run-up on Honshu, from which the amount of slip on the fault could be estimated. Their conclusion: the quake was at least magnitude 9 and perhaps as big as magnitude 9.3, making it as large as any on Earth.

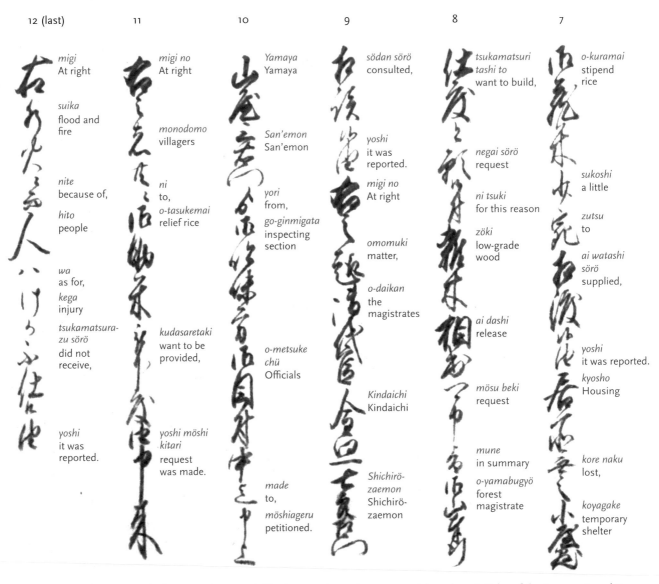

12 (last)

migi
At right

suika
flood and fire

nite
because of,

hito
people

wa
as for,
kega
injury

tsukamatsura-zu sörö
did not receive,

yoshi
it was reported.

11

migi no
At right

monodomo
villagers

ni
to,
o-tasukemai
relief rice

kudasaretaki
want to be provided,

yoshi möshi kitari
request was made.

10

Yamaya
Yamaya

San'emon
San'emon

yori
from,
go-ginmigata
inspecting section

o-metsuke chü
Officials

made
to,
möshiageru
petitioned.

9

södan sörö
consulted,

yoshi
it was reported.

migi no
At right

omomuki
matter,

o-daikan
the magistrates

Kindaichi
Kindaichi

Shichirö-zaemon
Shichirö-zaemon

8

tsukamatsuri tashi to
want to build,

negai sörö
request

ni tsuki
for this reason

zöki
low-grade wood

ai dashi
release

mösu beki
request

mune
in summary
o-yamabugyö
forest magistrate

7

o-kuramai
stipend rice

sukoshi
a little

zutsu
to

ai watashi sörö
supplied,

yoshi
it was reported.

kyosho
Housing

kore naku
lost,

koyagake
temporary shelter

Japanese written record of AD 1700 tsunami. Twelve cursive columns provide a description of the tsunami and its aftermath in Kuwagaski, on the island of Honshu about 480 km north of Tokyo. The Japanese symbols were applied with a brush. Roman letters to the right provide a guide to the spoken Japanese (light brown). Literal translations follow in blue. The columns proceed from right to left and top to bottom. Matter already mentioned

Column 1 (first)

一 [start of entry]

Miyako
Miyako

o-daikansho
district
magistrate's
Office

no uchi
within,

Kuwagasaki-
mura
Kuwagasaki
village

nite
in,

saru
past

yōka
eighth day

2

no
of

yoru
night

kokonotsu-
doki
hour of nine,

tsunami
tsunami

uchiyose
came.

shosho no
Here and
there,

monodomo
villagers

yamayama
hills

e
to

3

nige mösu
escaped.

ato nite
Afterwards

shukka
started
fire

iekazu
number
of houses

nijikken
20 houses

shöshitsu
burned.

hoka ni
In addition,

4

jūsan-ken
13 houses

nami
waves

ni
by

uchiyaburare
sörö
were
destroyed,

yoshi
it was reported.

suika
Flood and fire

ichido
at the
same time

shuttai
happened.

sho
Various

5

dögu
belongings

wa
as for,

mösu ni
oyoba zu
needless
to say

nani nitemo
everything

issai
at all

ai-dashi
save

mösa-zu
could not.

6

sassoku
Soon
after,

katsumei
ni oyobi
sörö
became
famished

ni tsuki
thereby

hitokazu
number
of people,

hyaku-
gojü-kyü
nin
159 people

e
to,

therefore appears "at right" (9, 11, 12). Verbs end sentences; nouns follow all their modifiers; prepositions follow their objects. The written record states that the tsunami arrived at night (column 2); villagers fled to high ground (2–3); the water destroyed 13 houses (4) and set off a fire than burned 20 more (3); in response, magistrates in nearby Miyako issued rice to 159 persons (6–7) and sought wood for shelters (8–9); they kept other officials informed of their emergency efforts (9–12).

Mainly cloudy
Details, C28

THE Province

60¢

Coin box: 75¢
Outside Lower
Mainland:
$1 minimum

Thursday, March 1, 2001   Vancouver, B.C   www.theprovince.com

EIGHT-PAGE SPECIAL REPORT STARTS ON A2

QUAKE!

Powerful earthquake causes billions of dollars in damage to Seattle, and scares southern B.C.

— Reuters

Kristi Heim reacts to a crushed car and a collapsed wall at the Starbucks corporate headquarters building in Seattle yesterday.

The 2001 Nisqually earthquake, which had an epicentre south of Seattle — a wake-up call for residents of the Pacific Northwest.

Temblors of a Different Kind
Earthquakes close to our cities

The history of any one part of the earth, like the life of a soldier,
consists of long periods of boredom and short periods of terror.
— D.V. Ager *The nature of the stratigraphical record*
(Third edition, 1993)

T O THIS POINT, we have focused on subduction earthquakes, the great quakes triggered by rupture of the locked "megathrust" fault separating the North America and Juan de Fuca plates. This fault, or more correctly, fault zone, lies at considerable depth in the crust beneath our feet and only reaches the Earth's surface at the toe of the continental slope, on average about 110 kilometres off the coast.

In contrast, most faults within the North America plate extend to the surface on land. Some of these faults pose a considerable threat, as they are capable of generating earthquakes of magnitude 7 or larger and may occur within or close to some of our cities. Quakes of this size also can originate deeper in the Earth, within the subducting Juan de Fuca plate. Although magnitude 7 earthquakes release about 1000 times less energy than a magnitude 9 quake, the former could be devastating if their epicentres were within or very close to one or more of our communities. Many earth scientists are currently trying to determine which of the many faults in the Pacific Northwest are active and capable of spawning large earthquakes.

This chapter describes what is known of Cascadia's earthquakes based on recorded historic events, the progress that has been made in understanding these events, and associated risk implications.

Historical earthquakes

Interactions among the Juan de Fuca, Pacific, and North America plates are responsible for all earthquakes in the Pacific Northwest. Most earthquakes occur at plate boundaries and along transform faults segmenting **Juan de Fuca Ridge**. The Queen Charlotte fault, which separates the Pacific and North America plates and lies at the foot of the continental slope off the Queen Charlotte Islands, is the source of many of these quakes, including small ones that occur almost daily. It is a strike-slip fault, similar to the San

Epicentres of earthquakes in the Pacific Northwest from 1985 to 2004. The red dots are epicentres of quakes with sources in the subducting Juan de Fuca plate. The blue dots are epicentres of quakes centred in the overriding North America plate.

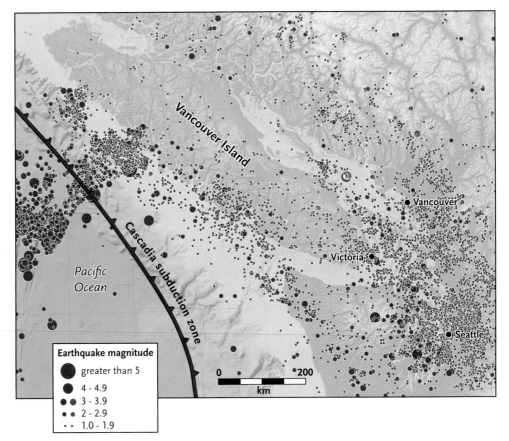

Andreas fault in California, although it lies offshore whereas most of the San Andreas fault is on land. The largest historical earthquake in Canada (magnitude 8.1) ruptured a 500-kilometre length of the Queen Charlotte fault on August 22, 1949. Smaller, magnitude 7 earthquakes occurred on the fault in 1929 and 1970.

The region just west of Vancouver Island is one of intense earthquake activity. More than one hundred earthquakes of magnitude 5 or greater have occurred there in the past 80 years. Epicentres extend northeasterly across the ocean floor from Juan de Fuca Ridge towards northern Vancouver Island along the Nootka fault, which separates the Juan de Fuca plate from the small Explorer plate to the north. Many earthquakes also occur within the Explorer plate, indicating that it, like its counterpart, the Gorda plate to the south, is being internally deformed. Earthquakes up to magnitude 6.8 have been recorded along transform faults segmenting Juan de Fuca Ridge, such as the **Sovanco** and **Blanco fracture zones**. The thinness and high temperature of the oceanic crust of the Juan de Fuca plate place an upper limit of about magnitude 7 on earthquakes that occur within it.

Shallow and deep: two big earthquakes in the Pacific Northwest

A magnitude 7.3 earthquake severely shook southwestern British Columbia on the morning of June 23, 1946. The earthquake occurred at a depth of 30 kilometres within continental crust, northwest of Courtenay on Vancouver Island. Although the quake was widely felt throughout British Columbia, damage was limited because the area near the epicentre where the most violent shaking occurred was sparsely populated. In towns nearest the epicentre, including Cumberland and Courtenay, chimneys fell, windows broke, and walls cracked. Roads and water and utility lines were also damaged. The earthquake triggered hundreds of small landslides. Were a comparable earthquake to occur today in the vicinity of Vancouver or Victoria, damage would likely be in the billions of dollars.

A large earthquake struck the southern Puget Lowland on February 28, 2001. The quake had a magnitude of 6.9 and was centred 52 kilometres below the Earth's surface, within the subducting oceanic plate. Its epicentre was in the vicinity of the Nisqually River delta in southern Puget Sound, 17 kilometres northeast of Olympia and 57 kilometres southwest of Seattle. It caused about $2 billion dollars (2006 dollars) in damage to roads, bridges, and buildings, destroyed 110 houses, seriously damaged another 126, and cut off power to 17,000 households. This earthquake was only slightly smaller than the quake that devastated Kobe, Japan in January 1995. The Kobe quake claimed 5500 lives and caused over $200 billion in damage and other economic losses.

Why did the Kobe and Nisqually earthquakes, both in heavily populated areas, have such dramatically different effects? One reason may be that buildings and other engineered structures in the Pacific Northwest have been designed and constructed to withstand the shaking of magnitude 6 and 7 earthquakes. A more important reason, however, is that the Nisqually earthquake occurred sufficiently deep in the Earth that the intensity of the seismic waves had diminished before reaching the places where most people live. In contrast, the Kobe earthquake was a shallow crustal event; the fault rupture ran right through the city. Thus the seismic waves traveled only a short distance from the source before striking Kobe with full force.

In the region encompassing the Cascadia subduction zone, earthquakes occur both within the subducting oceanic plate (**in-slab earthquakes**) and in the overriding continental plate (upper **crustal earthquakes**). In-slab earthquakes are common beneath Puget Lowland and the southernmost Strait of Georgia and are caused by pressure-induced mineral changes within the rocks and by flexure of the subducting plate as it steepens towards the mantle.

Section of the Earth's crust through southern Vancouver Island and the northern tip of Olympic Peninsula showing sources of earthquakes within the North America plate (blue dots) and Juan de Fuca plate (red dots). No earthquake foci are known from the boundary between the two plates. White arrows show relative directions of plate motion.

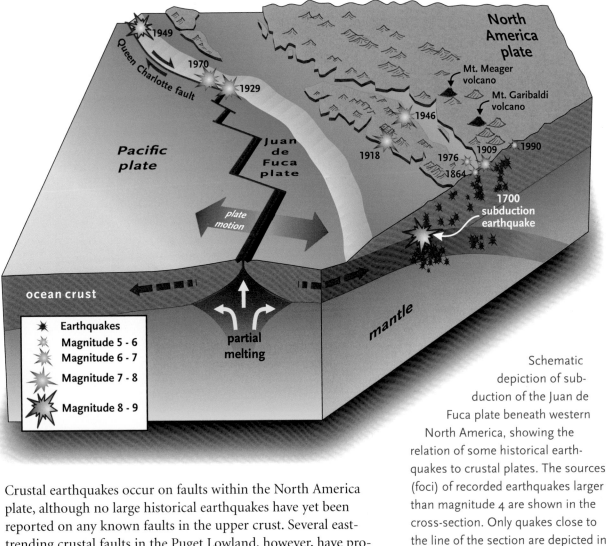

Schematic depiction of subduction of the Juan de Fuca plate beneath western North America, showing the relation of some historical earthquakes to crustal plates. The sources (foci) of recorded earthquakes larger than magnitude 4 are shown in the cross-section. Only quakes close to the line of the section are depicted in the cross-section. The epicentres, or points on the Earth directly above the quake foci, are shown on the surface of the diagram. Only moderate to large earthquakes (magnitude 5 or greater) are depicted on the surface.

Crustal earthquakes occur on faults within the North America plate, although no large historical earthquakes have yet been reported on any known faults in the upper crust. Several east-trending crustal faults in the Puget Lowland, however, have produced large prehistoric earthquakes (pages 101 to 104). The largest historical earthquakes on Vancouver Island occurred in 1918 and 1946. The epicentre of the 1918 earthquake was near Hesquiat Peninsula on the west coast of Vancouver Island. It had a magnitude of 7.2 and occurred at a depth of about 15 kilometres, within continental crust. The 1946 quake, of magnitude 7.3, was centred

Some significant earthquakes in the Pacific Northwest

Date	Location	Magnitude	Comment
January 26, 1700	West of Vancouver Island	ca. 9	Great earthquake; native villages destroyed
December 15, 1872	North-central Washington	7.4	Felt strongly
January 11, 1909	San Juan Islands	6	Deep, felt strongly
December 6, 1918	Vancouver Island	7	Damage on west coast of Vancouver Island
January 24, 1920	San Juan Islands	5.5	Deep, felt strongly
June 23, 1946	Vancouver Island	7.3	Much damage on central Vancouver Island
April 13, 1949	Puget Lowland	7	Deep, much damage in Seattle and Tacoma
April 29, 1965	Puget Lowland	6.5	Deep, much damage in Seattle
November 30, 1975	Strait of Georgia	4.9	Shallow, many aftershocks
May 16, 1976	Southern Gulf Islands	5.4	Deep
April 14, 1990	Fraser Lowland	4.9	Shallow, many aftershocks
February 28, 2001	Puget Lowland (Nisqually)	6.9	Deep, much damage in Seattle and Olympia

about 25 kilometres northwest of Courtenay at a depth of about 30 kilometres, also within continental crust. Widespread damage was done to chimneys at several localities throughout the central part of Vancouver Island during the latter event. Liquefaction disrupted beaches along both coasts, and the ground subsided in places up to about 9 centimetres on the east coast of the island. A poorly documented crustal earthquake near Lake Chelan in the North Cascades in 1872 is thought to be the largest seismic event in the Pacific Northwest since settlement of the region, with an estimated magnitude of 7.4.

Three earthquakes of magnitude 6.5 to 7 have occurred in Puget Lowland during the last 60 years. The most recent of these events was the Nisqually earthquake (magnitude 6.9), which occurred on February 28, 2001, and was centred 57 kilometres southwest of Seattle. All three earthquakes were in-slab events and thus had deep foci (30 to 60 kilometres) within a Wadati-Benioff zone that steepens from 10 to 12 degrees beneath the Olympic Peninsula to as much as 20 degrees under Puget Sound.

Upper crustal earthquakes up to magnitude 5 that have been

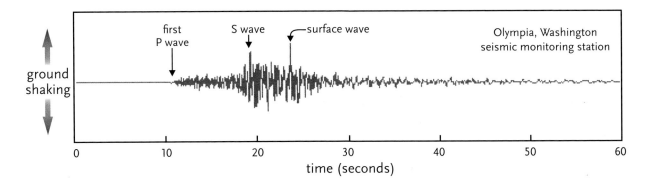

ground shaking

first P wave

S wave

surface wave

Olympia, Washington seismic monitoring station

time (seconds)

recorded in south-coastal British Columbia, Washington, and Oregon are caused by compressive forces directed to the northeast. Geophysicists think that the compressive stresses result from a slow, clockwise rotation of continental crust beneath western Washington, which is being driven by oblique convergence of the Juan de Fuca plate relative to the edge of the continent. The slowly rotating crustal block is buttressed to the north by Vancouver Island and the southern Coast Mountains, causing it to compress and occasionally rupture along east-trending faults.

Out of the sea 1000 years ago

Near Restoration Point on Bainbridge Island in Puget Sound, a flat wave-cut terrace extends from the present shore up to 300 metres inland, where it abruptly terminates against a steeply rising slope (see diagram, next page). This feature is thought to be an intertidal rock platform that was elevated above sea level at some time in the past. The interpretation is supported by the presence of a similar rock platform that extends offshore from the beach just east of Restoration Point and is forming today due to erosion by waves and currents. The full significance of the elevated rock platform was not realized until around 1990 when Robert Bucknam of the U.S. Geological Survey cored a small pond behind what he interpreted to be an ancient gravel spit that had formed when the rock

Seismogram of the February 2001 Nisqually earthquake recorded near Olympia, Washington. The earthquake had a magnitude of 6.9 and caused about $2 billion damage (2006 dollars). The "zero" second mark indicates the beginning of the earthquake at the source. The amplitude of the squiggles on the graph is proportional to the intensity of the shaking.

Radar (LIDAR) image of part of Bainbridge Island in Puget Sound (top). The image accurately depicts the ground surface with vegetation removed. The dashed red line shows the trace of the Seattle fault. Slip along the fault about 1000 years ago raised a wave-cut terrace 7 metres above sea level (bottom right).

platform lay within the tidal zone. The pond today is accumulating fine-grained freshwater sediments, which Bob recovered in his cores. Below the freshwater sediments, however, are brackish-water, intertidal sediments deposited at a time when the pond was directly connected to Puget Sound. What interested Bucknam was the contact between the intertidal and freshwater sediments in his cores. It was razor sharp, indicating that the depositional environment had suddenly changed. Initial carbon dating of fossil plants in the core showed that the sudden change occurred sometime between 500 and 1700 years ago. Subsequent dating at other sites has yielded a more precise age of about AD 1000 for the event. In 1992, Bucknam and several colleagues suggested that the change resulted from sudden uplift of the former intertidal platform to its present elevation seven metres above sea level during an earthquake on a nearby structure that they named the Seattle fault. The earthquake likely had a magnitude of about 7. Bucknam and his colleague Sam Johnson later traced the fault east across Bainbridge Island and Puget Sound and through Seattle using geophysical data.

The earthquake must have been accompanied by very strong ground shaking, but it had other effects. The seafloor was propelled upward where the fault crosses Puget Sound between Bainbridge Island and Seattle. The sudden uplift of the ocean floor triggered a tsunami that raced north and south along Puget Sound and even into Hood Canal. The waves surged across low-lying areas bordering the sound, leaving a distinctive layer of sand in its wake. The earthquake also triggered landslides that carried trees into Lake Washington that have been recovered and dated to the time of the earthquake.

These discoveries changed the way the Washington state government views seismic risk, because they showed that a destructive, shallow, crustal earthquake of the 1995 Kobe type in Japan could occur very close to, or within, Seattle. When Bucknam and colleagues published their findings, this earthquake was thought to be a unique event, but subsequent research has shown that other earthquakes have occurred on the Seattle fault.

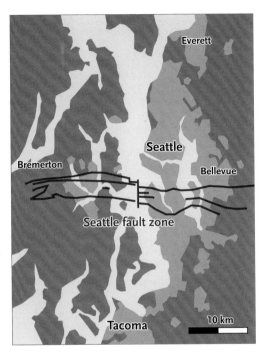

Surface traces of the fault strands that form the Seattle fault zone. Any of these faults could produce a large earthquake that would seriously damage Seattle.

Layer of tsunami sand exposed in the wall of a drainage ditch at Cultus Bay at the south end of Whidbey Island in Puget Sound. A tsunami left a sheet of sand in the Cultus Bay marsh following a large earthquake on the Seattle fault about 1000 years ago.

LIDAR: *A new tool for the earthquake detective*

In the past few years, a powerful tool has been added to the toolbox that geologists use to search for past earthquakes. This tool is LIDAR, an acronym for Laser Infrared Detection Aperture Radar, and it works as follows. Radar pulses are transmitted from airborne instruments to the ground and reflected back to the aircraft. Each pulse is precisely located in three-dimensional space using high-precision satellite technology. Millions of pulses are transmitted as the plane tracks back and forth across a survey area. After the flight, the data are processed to provide an image of the surface that reflected the radar energy. Some energy is reflected from the tops of trees and other vegetation, but most of it bounces off the ground. The vegetation reflectors can be removed during data processing to provide a crisp and detailed image of the Earth's surface. The Seattle fault stands out very clearly on a LIDAR image, whereas it can scarcely be seen on conventional aerial photographs because it

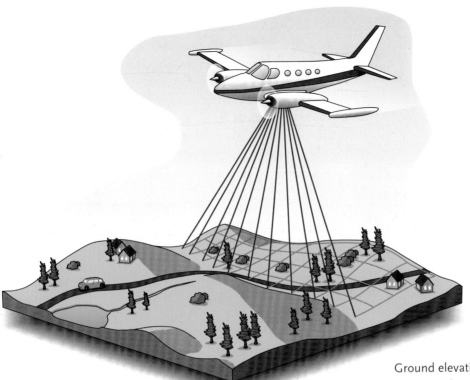

Ground elevation data are acquired with an airborne LIDAR imaging system. The LIDAR instrument transmits and receives millions of radar pulses every minute, allowing a precise three-dimensional map of the ground surface to be made.

crosses forested terrain. By using this technique, scientists are able to see and map features that are normally hidden to the eye or other conventional methods.

Over the last five years, LIDAR imagery has been acquired for much of Puget Lowland under a cooperative arrangement between the United States and local governments and industry. Faults previously only suspected of being active are clearly visible cutting the surface in LIDAR images. They locally disrupt sediments that are less than a few thousand years old and thus have slipped once or more during that time. The imagery provides another benefit: because the locations of the faults are now known, geologists can closely study the structures to unravel their history. They have done this by digging trenches across the surface traces of the faults and studying the exposed sediments.

Trenches and temblors

Trench digging is not a high-tech skill, but appropriately placed trenches can yield a wealth of information on the recent history of a fault. Geologists choose sites for trenching carefully. The trench must straddle the fault being investigated; it must be dug in an area where the water table is below the floor of the trench; and it should extend through earth materials that accumulated in the recent geological past, that is, in the last 10,000 years or so. The last point is important because the geologist is looking for evidence that sedimentary layers have been broken or deformed by movement along the fault and that the dislocation occurred recently. If the displaced material is 10 million years old, for example, all we can infer is that the fault ruptured sometime in the last 10 million years – not very helpful to those responsible for planning! However, if the displaced material is only 500 years old, the fault must have slipped less than 500 years ago, a conclusion that is relevant to planners. It's even better if the sedimentary layers span a long period, say from the present back 10,000 years. In such a case, a series of earthquakes might be inferred from cross-cutting relationships between sediment layers and the fault strands that dislocate them.

Drawing of sediment layers exposed in the wall of a trench excavated to document prehistoric earthquakes. The lowest, oldest layers of sediment in the trench are broken and displaced by numerous faults (red lines), recording sudden movements during at least one earthquake. In contrast, the upper sediment layers are not displaced by the faults and, therefore, must be younger than the earthquake that broke the underlying layers. The approximate time of the earthquake can be determined from the ages of the two sets of strata.

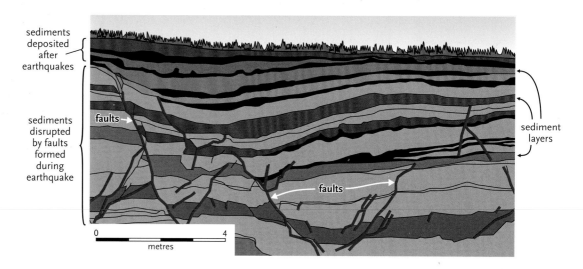

sediments deposited after earthquakes

sediments disrupted by faults formed during earthquake

faults

faults

sediment layers

0   4

metres

Trenches are excavated with back-hoes or shovels, sometimes to a depth of 5 metres below the surface. They have vertical sides and some need shoring with timbers to prevent collapse of the walls. Digging the trench is the easy part; it is followed by painstaking description and mapping of the geological features exposed in the trench walls. The ages of earthquakes are determined by carbon dating fossils such as plant debris, bones, and charcoal recovered from fault-disrupted sediments exposed in the trench walls. Additional information on fault history can be gleaned from natural exposures of sediments, for example coastal bluffs along Puget Sound and the Strait of Georgia.

Such investigations have provided good evidence for multiple large earthquakes along the Seattle fault, the South Whidbey Island fault, and other east-west trending structures in Puget Lowland. Collectively, the data indicate that Puget Lowland has a long history of big quakes. These large earthquakes are not randomly distributed through the region but are concentrated along several active faults.

Fault trenching has not yet been done on the populated south coast of British Columbia for several reasons. One is that LIDAR images, which are essential for picking good sites for trenching, are not yet available for areas around the Strait of Georgia. A second reason is that there is not enough money for such seismic hazard research in Canada. A third is that no definitely active faults have yet been found in the Vancouver and Victoria metropolitan areas.

This trench in the southern Coast Mountains near Pemberton, British Columbia, was dug to determine the history of movement of a fault. The surface trace of the fault is marked by a conspicuous scarp that extends for several kilometres along the flank and crest of a ridge near Mount Currie. The trench, excavated using pick and shovels, extends across the fault scarp and exposes earth materials less than 15,000 years old that have been displaced by vertical movements along the fault.

Potentially active faults in southern British Columbia

As described on previous pages, several of Cascadia's crustal faults, including the Seattle and South Whidbey Island faults, may rupture following a great Cascadia subduction earthquake, as in Japan with faults that are dynamically associated with plate-boundary rupture at the Nankai subduction zone. Alternatively, these faults may generate earthquakes that are independent of activity at the plate boundary.

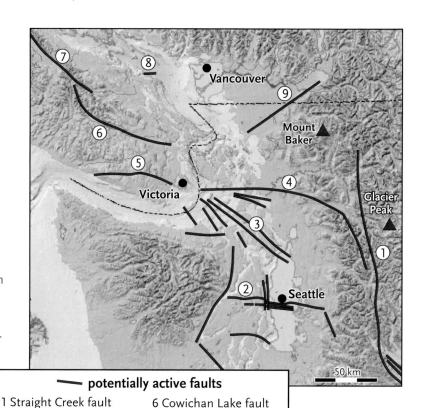

Locations of some of the faults in northwest Washington and southwest British Columbia that could produce large earthquakes.

— **potentially active faults**

1 Straight Creek fault
2 Seattle fault
3 South Whidbey Is. fault
4 Devils Mountain fault
5 Leech River fault
6 Cowichan Lake fault
7 Beaufort Range fault
8 Strait of Georgia fault
9 Vedder fault

Several other crustal faults may be active, but have not yet been proven to be. An example is the Leech River fault, which extends across southern Vancouver Island and through Greater Victoria. This fault, if extrapolated southeast across Juan de Fuca Strait and the northern end of Puget Sound, may connect to the South Whidbey Island fault, which is known to be active. Geophysical surveys in Juan de Fuca Strait have revealed dislocations of the sea floor across the extension of the Leech River fault and the Devils Mountain fault. The Leech River fault is an impressive landscape feature. It follows the valleys of Loss Creek, Bear Creek, and lower Leech River, and forms the boundary between different pieces of crust that make up southern Vancouver Island. Until recently, the last movement on the Leech River fault was thought to have been no younger that about 42 million years ago. However, the fault's striking topographic expression and its possible relation to the South Whidbey Island fault suggest that it may have been active much more recently, possibly within the past few thousand years.

Another possible active fault is the Vedder fault, which extends northeast from the state of Washington into British Columbia along the south side of Sumas Prairie. It, like the Leech River fault, is an ancient rupture, but its strikingly youthful appearance suggests recent movement. The Portland Hills fault, which traverses the city of Portland, is another possibly active fault. Recently discovered geological evidence shows that the fault has slipped within the past 10,000 years.

Since the first seismographs were installed on southern Vancouver Island and in the Lower Mainland of British

The valley of Loss Creek on southern Vancouver Island, beneath which two different pieces of crust, the Crescent and Pacific Rim terranes, are separated by the northward-inclined Leech River fault.

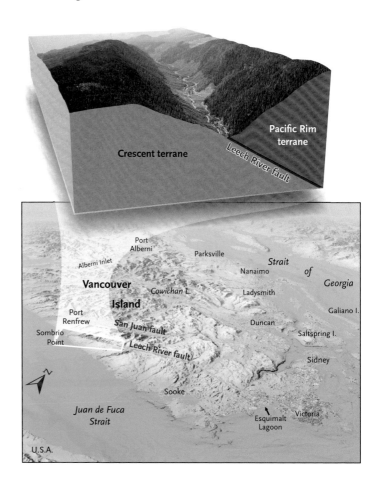

Andrée Blais-Stevens

Columbia, no foci have been located on known faults, although a great number of crustal earthquakes occur in these regions. This apparent contradiction may be historically due to an insufficient number of seismographs to precisely locate foci. However, the same situation prevails today, even with an expanded network of more sophisticated instruments. Many earthquakes in the upper crust may occur along unmapped "blind faults" that do not reach the surface or along new, unrecognized faults.

We do know that a large, potentially destructive crustal earthquake can occur close to Vancouver and Victoria, because geological evidence of such quakes has been found near these cities. Sediment cores recovered from the floor of Saanich Inlet, just north of Victoria, contain many debris flow layers that Andrée Blais-Stevens of the Geological Survey of Canada interpreted to be products of large earthquakes. Careful dating of the cores has shown that a few of the debris flows probably occurred during great subduction zone earthquakes, but that most were likely triggered by local, moderate to strong quakes. The Saanich Inlet cores record one such event every 150 years on average, back at least 2000 years.

The Hard Hand
of Nature
Earthquake damage

Destruction, hence, like creation, is one of Nature's mandates.
— Marquis de Sade, *Philosophy in the Bedroom* (1795)

EARTHQUAKES CAN CAUSE sudden and enormous damage. Unlike raging forest fires and floods, which develop over a few days or weeks, thus allowing evacuation of people and the organization of relief efforts, earthquakes strike without warning and complete their damage within just a few minutes. The moderate (magnitude 6.6) earthquake at Bam in southeast Iran on December 26, 2003, left over 26,000 people dead and this ancient city in ruins all in less time than it takes to wash your hands. Shock and trauma immobilize survivors, and it may take several days before municipal, provincial, state, and federal authorities can estimate the extent and kinds of damage and mobilize a relief effort.

This chapter describes the kinds of damage that are directly and indirectly associated with earthquakes. Damage is caused directly by strong ground shaking and indirectly by secondary effects such as ground rupture, liquefaction, landslides, sudden changes in land elevation, and seiches. Also important are the resulting fires, flooding, and the spread of disease through contamination or destruction of water supplies. And, finally, some earthquakes centred offshore, such as along the Cascadia subduction zone, generate massive sea waves called tsunamis. Tsunamis are so interesting and have such enormous energy and destructive power that we devote a separate chapter to them.

Ground shaking

Ground shaking is the signature characteristic of earthquakes and is responsible for most quake damage. It is also terrifying. Anyone who was close to the epicentre of the Northridge earthquake in 1994, the Kobe earthquake in 1995, or the Loma Prieta earthquake in 1989, for example, will tell you that the 30 seconds or so of strong

shaking they experienced were the most frightening moments of their lives. The mind simply cannot grasp the reality that "terra firma" is jumping up and down or sideways, or rolling like waves at sea. In an exceptionally strong earthquake, lateral and vertical movements may be so strong that objects on the ground can become temporarily suspended in air and a person cannot stand. After the great (magnitude 9.5) earthquake in Chile in 1960, the engine of a train was found undamaged and upright sitting beside the tracks on which it had rested. The train was momentarily suspended in air during the earthquake, while the tracks below it shifted sideways. The terror that a person feels during an earthquake is compounded by noise, for earthquakes are not quiet. Part of the energy released during an earthquake moves through the air and can be heard:

The 1994 Kobe earthquake damaged and destroyed many buildings in the city. The top photo shows a "pancaked" seven-floor building. A building in the bottom photo collapsed into the street, starting a fire.

The noise emanates from the basement of time, a
Cyclopean orchestra tuning instruments. It rolls in on a
basso profundo roar. During Loma Prieta, it began with a
sonorous, bottom-octave moan, steadily blending with the
sound of things straining, fracturing, cracking, settling,
popping, and shattering; but what I remember most vividly
is the grinding, the unearthly noise of great surfaces and
structures grating together. [Marc Reisner describing the
noise of the 1989 earthquake in San Francisco; *A*
Dangerous Place, p. 103].

Most people in the Pacific Northwest are familiar with earthquake noise. A short pop or bang is commonly heard during
many small quakes in the region. The sharp noise is produced by
compressional waves (page 37), which, upon reaching the Earth's
surface, suddenly compress the air. The air then rapidly expands,
producing the noise.

The complex character of seismic ground motions makes it
difficult to predict damage to structures from an earthquake of a
given magnitude. Seismic design requirements for buildings arise
from government building codes and are based on peak velocities
and horizontal accelerations of the ground for earthquakes of a
range of magnitudes. They take into account **seismic attenuation**,
which is the rate at which the intensity of ground motion decreases
away from the epicentre. The velocity and acceleration values in
our building codes have been estimated with strong-motion
instruments placed near earthquake epicentres.

Ground shaking depends not only on magnitude and distance
from the hypocentre, but also on local geology and topography.
Shaking may be far more severe in areas of loose, soft sediments
than in adjacent areas of firm ground (**amplification**, see figure,
next page). A person in one part of a city could experience shaking
several times more intense than another person as little as a kilometre away. Ground motion amplification has long been recognized
from damage patterns of historical earthquakes. For example, most
of the chimneys in Port Alberni that were damaged during the 1946
central Vancouver Island earthquake were in parts of the town

located on thick silt and clay. Houses built on rock suffered little damage. More dramatic damage due to ground motion amplification occurred in Mexico City during the 1985 Michoacan earthquake (pages 63 to 65) and in San Francisco during the 1989 Loma Prieta earthquake. In the former case, the dominant period of the long-period seismic waves matched the natural period of the thick lake clays underlying Mexico City, causing an amplification that shook many high buildings apart, killing 8000 people. Only buildings of a particular height range were affected. Taller and shorter buildings were much less damaged. Low buildings, including old churches with delicate exterior artwork, were not affected at all, because the higher frequency waves that would have damaged them had completely attenuated between the hypocentre and the city.

Studies of damage caused by the strong shaking of the 2004 Sumatra earthquake suggest that a Cascadia megathrust earthquake could affect a larger area than previously thought. Many factors influence the extent and effects of shaking, including the type of building construction, seismic wave attenuation, and local geology, but the Sumatra earthquake showed that subduction earthquakes can cause structural damage over a very large area.

The severity of ground motion during an earthquake depends on the thickness and physical properties of geological materials. Tall buildings located on thick unconsolidated sediments, such as river deltas, will be more strongly shaken than those lying directly on bedrock because low-frequency, long-period seismic waves are amplified as they pass through the thick sediment pile. Tall buildings resonate with these low-frequency seismic waves, whereas small structures do not (left). In contrast, low buildings located on 10 to 20 metres of unconsolidated sediments may be more strongly shaken than those on bedrock because high-frequency, short-period seismic waves are commonly amplified in these thinner sediments. Low buildings resonate with the high-frequency waves, whereas tall structures do not (centre).

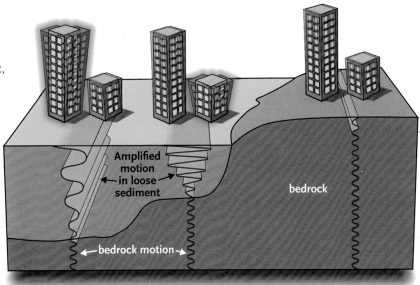

Amplified motion in loose sediment

bedrock

bedrock motion

Soft deposits of silt and clay susceptible to ground motion amplification are common in British Columbia, Washington, and Oregon, especially in populated areas. Thick deposits of silt and clay dating to the end of the **Ice Age** about 12,000 years ago underlie lowlands bordering the Strait of Georgia, Juan de Fuca Strait, Puget Sound, and in the Willamette Valley in Oregon. Younger silt- and clay-rich sediments also underlie large, urbanized deltas and **floodplains,** including those of the Fraser River and the rivers flowing from the Cascade Range in Washington.

Ground rupture

As mentioned previously, an earthquake is caused by the rapid movement of rocks along a fault. The ground will rupture, or break, when this movement extends to the surface. Ground rupture can seriously damage bridges, highways, rail beds, utility and transmission lines, dams, and other structures that cross the fault. Fault rupture zones may be very narrow (less than a metre), or tens or hundreds of metres wide. Surface rupture is common during large earthquakes in some areas of California, mainly along strike-slip faults where hypocentres are relatively shallow. Although no earthquake in the coastal Pacific Northwest is known to have breached the surface during the last 100 years, there is clear evidence of this having happened in the recent geologic past at several places in the Puget Lowland.

Following the very damaging San Fernando earthquake in 1971, the State of California passed legislation requiring that a geological site investigation be completed in "special study zones," encompassing the rupture zones of potentially and recently active faults. The purpose of the legislation is to determine whether an active fault passes through a proposed building site. The special study zones and the faults on which they are based are shown on special maps. This approach might be useful in Washington, Oregon, and British Columbia because several potentially active faults have been identified there.

Liquefaction

Earthquake shaking can transform loose, water-saturated silts and sands into fluid material through the process of liquefaction. As water-saturated sediment is shaken, the individual grains attempt to move towards one another into a tighter packing arrangement. Water in the space between the grains, however, does not have time to escape. The intergranular water pressure increases rapidly, and the grains in effect become suspended in the pore water. At that instant, the sediment is no longer a solid but rather behaves as a fluid. This process is similar to what you see when you repeatedly pat your hand on wet sand at the beach.

Release of the high water pressure causes liquefied silt and sand to move upward along cracks in the ground and erupt onto the surface to form sand volcanoes. Liquefaction may also trigger **lateral spreads**, whereby slabs of cohesive sediment move sideways towards the walls of river channels or delta fronts, cracking in the process. At depth, the liquefied sediment loses its strength and can no longer support structures built on it. Buildings may sink or lean, or their foundations may crack due to irregular settling or horizontal movement. Materials most likely to liquefy include landfill and poorly compacted sand and silt along the coast and beneath deltas and river plains. An area of particular concern is the Fraser River delta. A thick layer of liquefiable wet sand lies beneath a capping layer of silt and peat throughout much of the delta plain. Geologists have found evidence on the delta of liquefaction triggered by a large prehistoric earthquake about 1700 years ago. The evidence includes sand volcanoes, clastic dykes, and buckling and displacement of the ground. Furthermore, engineering tests have shown that the buried sand will liquefy if strongly shaken during a future earthquake.

Most large historical earthquakes, including those in the Pacific Northwest, have been accompanied by liquefaction. A spectacular

Damage to apartment buildings in Niigata, Japan, caused by liquefaction during a strong earthquake on June 16, 1964. About a third of the city subsided as much as 2 metres due to liquefaction.

example occurred during a strong earthquake at Port Royal, the first British settlement on Jamaica, on June 7, 1692. The town, housing 6500 souls, was built on a sand spit extending across the mouth of Kingston Harbour. Violent ground shaking liquefied the spit, causing it to flow into the harbour. Much of the town sank several metres into the soft sand. Other well known examples include the 1964 Niigata earthquake (magnitude 7.3) in Japan and the 1811–1812 New Madrid earthquakes (magnitude 8) in the U.S. mid-continent region. Liquefaction caused severe damage to the Marina District of San Francisco during the Loma Prieta earthquake on October 17, 1989. The experience of the 1965 Seattle (magnitude 6.5) and 2001 Nisqually (magnitude 6.9) earthquakes has shown where liquefaction will occur during the next damaging quake in the Puget Lowland. Liquefaction can also be expected in Portland, Vancouver, Victoria, and other cities during a strong quake. Problem sites include some shorelines, areas of landfill, and low-lying areas near rivers.

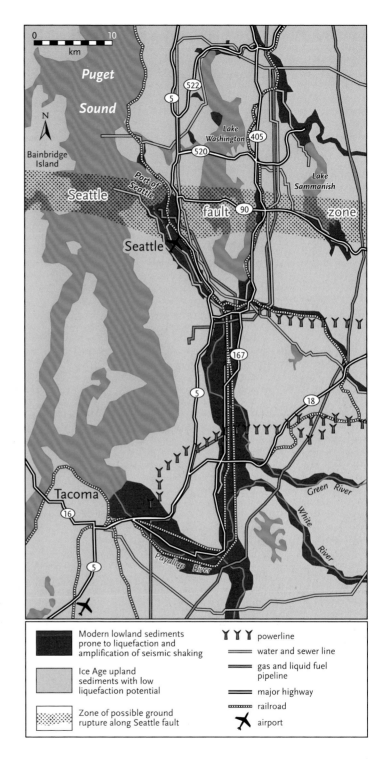

Earthquake hazard map of the Seattle area, with major infrastructure shown. The map shows areas that are susceptible to liquefaction and ground motion amplification, and the zone of possible ground rupture and displacement associated with the Seattle fault.

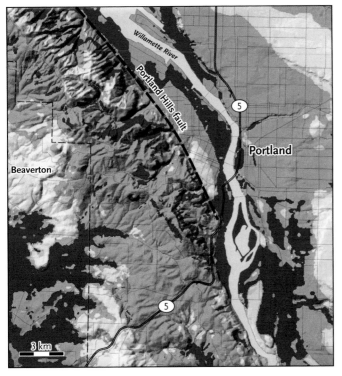

Earthquake hazard map of Portland, showing hazard areas on a three-dimensional shaded-relief map. Red areas, the zones of highest risk, are underlain by loose, water-saturated silt and sand.

Liquefaction susceptibility map of the Fraser Lowland. Damage due to liquefaction during an earthquake is most likely in the areas coloured red, which are underlain by water-saturated, loose, silty and sandy sediments and by landfill.

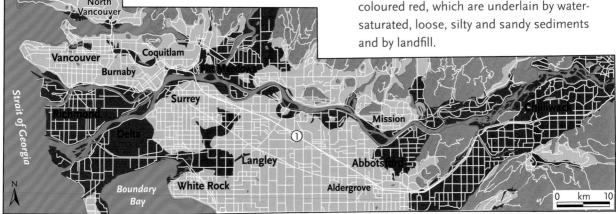

Risk of liquefaction during an earthquake

Moderate to high
(modern lowland sediments and landfill)

Low (Ice Age upland sediments)

None (bedrock)

Landslides

Landslides are a major cause of earthquake damage and death. They occur most commonly on steep ground underlain by loose sediment or unstable rock. More than half of the deaths caused by large earthquakes in Japan are the result of landslides, and the 1976 Guatemala earthquake triggered more than 10,000 landslides that claimed hundreds of lives and severely disrupted road and rail traffic. Closer to home, the 1946 central Vancouver Island earthquake caused several hundred small landslides, but the affected area was sparsely populated and so damage was minor.

Landslides are of particular concern in western North America because steep slopes are common there. Highways, rail lines, and power and natural gas lines pass through valleys and canyons bordered by steep, potentially unstable slopes. These lifelines can be blocked or severed by landslides. Examples of highways that are particularly vulnerable to landslides are the Trans-Canada Highway in the Fraser Canyon between Yale and Lillooet, the Sea-to-Sky Highway between West Vancouver and Pemberton, Highway 3 between Hope and Princeton, parts of the Coquihalla Highway, the Malahat Summit stretch of the Island Highway north of Victoria, parts of Highway 101 on the Olympic Peninsula and the Oregon coast, and parts of the several highways crossing the Cascade Range in Washington. Any steep slope of loose sediment or fractured rock, however, is vulnerable to failure during a strong earthquake, and structures must be sited and built with this possibility in mind.

A severe earthquake might cause many blockages over a large area, disrupting economic activity and restricting access to the affected region. In this context, even small landslides, which are the vast majority of those triggered by earthquakes, can be severely disruptive. The problem would be worse if the earthquake occurred during the rainy period when soils are saturated. An example of a landslide that would cause spectacular damage is a possible **rockslide** into the Fraser River in the Fraser Canyon at Hell's Gate. There, bedrock fractures parallel the steep east canyon wall, and small **rockfalls** are common. Road crews mitigate the problem by anchoring the rock with large bolts, installing drainage pipes, and removing loose rock from the slopes. But a strong earthquake could cause the entire canyon wall to collapse into the valley, damming the river and destroying the highway and transcontinental rail lines. The economic consequences of such an event would be enormous. A small rockslide occurred at Hell's Gate on February 23, 1914, during construction of the CN rail line, constricting the flow of the Fraser River and preventing a large run of salmon from reaching their spawning grounds. Millions of fish died before the blockage was cleared. The salmon runs during subsequent four-year periods were greatly reduced and have never rebounded to their 1914 level. The estimated accumulated loss to the Fraser River salmon fishery of this otherwise insignificant landslide is hundreds of millions of dollars.

Other areas of concern are deltas, such as those at the mouths of

Critical transportation corridors in the Lower Mainland of British Columbia that are at risk from earthquake-induced landslides. Some bridges and tunnels could also be damaged by ground shaking during a large earthquake.

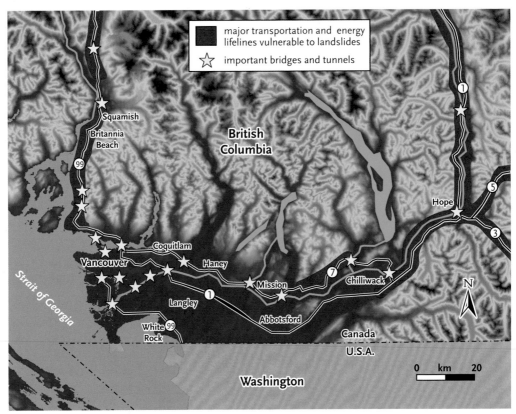

Aerial view of Deltaport at the western front of the Fraser delta northwest of Tsawwassen, British Columbia. This facility exports coal from mines in the Rocky Mountains to markets in Asia and is a major container terminal. Deltaport and the nearby Tsawwassen ferry terminal are located on thick deltaic sediments.

the Squamish, Fraser, and Skagit Rivers. Liquefaction of loose water-saturated sands and silts during an earthquake can cause landslides at the fronts of deltas and along river channels. Such ground failure is of great concern on the Fraser delta because of its large population and critical regional infrastructure, including a ferry terminal, the largest bulk loading facility in the Pacific Northwest, and the Vancouver International Airport.

The steep slopes of Cascade volcanoes are particularly unstable and can fail during earthquakes, volcanic eruptions, or severe rainstorms. Geologists have found abundant

Recent rockslide at Kennedy River on Vancouver Island. The blocky landslide debris plugged the river valley, forming a lake and drowning a forest.

evidence of large landslides on the flanks of all Cascade volcanoes, from Mount Meager on the north to Mount Lassen on the south. They have used this evidence to map areas at risk from landslides.

The greatest risk is to communities at the base of Mount Rainier, south of Seattle. Huge volcanic **debris flows**, consisting of cement-like slurries of mud, sand, boulders, and woody debris mixed with water derived from snow and ice, have flowed down the valleys that drain the summit of Mount Rainier onto the now-populated communities east of Tacoma and south of Seattle. The most recent of these debris flows, known as the "Electron Mudflow," happened about 600 years ago and covered what is now the town of Orting. A similar, but much larger debris flow, the "Osceola Mudflow," occurred about 5600 years ago. It had a volume of about 1 cubic kilometre and travelled at a speed of more than 80 kilometres per hour. The towns of Auburn, Buckley, Enumclaw, Puyallup, and Sumner are located on deposits of the Osceola Mudflow. If the same event were to occur today, property damage would be enormous and, barring adequate warning, the loss of life could be in the tens of thousands.

Rockfall on the Trans-Canada Highway in the Fraser Canyon near Yale.

Landslides, regardless of their cause, come in a variety of different forms and involve both rock and sediment. Rockfalls are the smallest but most common landslides in mountains. They occur when a mass of rock separates from a cliff and falls or tumbles onto the slope below. **Rock avalanches** are much larger but less common. They are sheet-like masses of blocky debris resulting from the failure of a large body of rock. The debris travels very rapidly, commonly far beyond the foot of the failed slope. Slumps are rotational landslides involving relatively intact sediment or rock that moves down slope on curved failure surfaces. Debris flows, often called "mud flows" by the popular press, are landslides that move in a fluid state. Most debris flows are derived from sediment; they contain abundant water and move at high velocities. Similar landslides containing little water are termed **debris avalanches** or debris slides. Lateral spreads involve the horizontal displacement of fractured but largely intact slabs of sediment on underlying liquefied or plastically deforming layers. During earthquakes, lateral spreading commonly occurs in areas where surface layers of silt and clay overlie loose, water-saturated sand.

The susceptibility of an area to landslides can be estimated by assessing slope steepness, local geology, and groundwater conditions. Locations of previous landslides also give clues as to where slopes are most likely to fail. Common sense dictates that steep slopes underlain by weak rocks are susceptible to landslides, and flat or gentle slopes with strong rocks are of no concern. A rigorous landslide susceptibility analysis should consider the possibility that earthquakes can trigger slope failure.

Land-level change

Large earthquakes can raise or lower the land, as much as several metres in extreme cases. **Coseismic** uplift or subsidence results from movement along a fault during the quake. Localized subsidence may also be caused by compaction or liquefaction of loose sediments, for example beneath floodplains and deltas.

Why is land-level change during an earthquake considered a hazard? Our coastal communities have been built on the assumption that the level of the sea will never change, aside from the daily ebb and flow of tides. We have constructed an elaborate coastal infrastructure at the margins of the Strait of Georgia, Puget Sound, and along the Pacific coast, assuming this to be the case. This infrastructure includes docks, wharves, ferry terminals, shoreline roads, and waterfront homes, collectively valued in the tens to hundreds of billions of dollars. What would happen if a large earthquake beneath Seattle, for example, lowered or raised the city one to two metres? If the land dropped this amount, development along the shoreline would be flooded, ecologically important tidal wetlands would be inundated, and shores currently vulnerable to erosion would, without protection, retreat under wave attack. If, on the other hand, the land rose one to two metres, the shoreline would move seaward in an instant, leaving some fixed coastal infrastructure "high and dry." Perhaps the worst thing about both of these scenarios is that the changes will not necessarily go away – Seattleites might be stuck with a coastal infrastructure out of sync with the post-earthquake sea.

Some comfort is provided by the fact that the largest historical earthquakes in British Columbia and Washington have produced only small changes (a few centimetres) in the elevation of the land, suggesting that coseismic subsidence and uplift are only minor hazards. This statement, however, should be qualified, because a large earthquake about 1000 years ago uplifted land on one side of the Seattle fault 7 metres and dropped land on the other side several metres. A similar, large earthquake at shallow depth could cause areas bordering Puget Sound or the Strait of Georgia to subside enough to flood or strand coastal development.

The west coast of Vancouver Island and the Pacific coast of Washington and Oregon could drop 1 to 2 metres during a great earthquake along the megathrust fault at the Cascadia subduction zone. This has happened many times during the last several thousand years, most recently in AD 1700. Subsidence of this amount would affect port facilities and other coastal development in towns such as Tofino, Ucluelet, Astoria, Seaside, and Newport.

Seiches

Seiches are oscillations in a lake, harbour, inlet, or other confined body of water. They are commonly produced by large earthquakes, when the frequency of the seismic waves corresponds to the natural frequency of oscillation of the water body. Water moves back and forth in its basin with gradually increasing amplitude, much as children slop water back and forth in a bathtub, until the seismic waves pass, and then oscillates with decreasing amplitude for some time.

Seiches can happen far beyond the felt area of an earthquake. The great Lisbon earthquake of 1755, for example, produced seiches throughout Europe, as far away as Scandinavia. Seiche waves in the harbour of Yarmouth, England, 1800 kilometres from Lisbon, were 2 metres high. The 1950 Assam (India) earthquake produced seiches in at least 37 lakes and **fjords** in Norway, with some waves more than one metre high. Seiches occurred in large lakes throughout North America and in the Gulf of Mexico following the great earthquake in Alaska in 1964.

Seiches may cause localized flooding and erosion, but do not often inflict serious damage. It is not known if any lakes or bays in the coastal Pacific Northwest would experience seiches during a large earthquake. However, a megathrust earthquake at the Cascadia subduction zone probably would produce seiches in many of the large lakes of the continental interior, such as Great Bear Lake, Great Slave Lake, Lake Athabasca, and possibly the Great Lakes.

Fire

Many large earthquakes trigger destructive fires. The San Francisco earthquake in 1906 ignited fires that burned 30,000 buildings in 520 square blocks, leaving 250,000 people homeless. At the time of that earthquake, most of San Francisco's buildings were constructed largely of wood. Many blazes started during the quake from debris on unattended stoves, sparks on leaking gas, and volatile chemicals. Most of the city's water supply system was disabled due to broken

Market Street in downtown San Francisco after the 1906 earthquake and fire. Wooden buildings, one to three stories high with brick or stone fronts, were interspersed with two- to eight-storey brick buildings. In this environment, the fire burned fiercely, and, in its aftermath, the streets were heaped with rubble to a depth of a metre or more.

pipes and mains. Consequently the fires spread rapidly through the wooden buildings. The fires became explosive and in three days engulfed the entire downtown area. Even ships in the harbour were set afire by flying embers.

Fortunately, a firestorm on that scale is unlikely to happen again in a North American city. No city now has the stock of wood buildings that San Francisco did in 1906, nor are structures as close to one another as they were in San Francisco at that time. More importantly, Victoria, Vancouver, Seattle, and other coastal communities have some capability of pumping water from the sea and using aerial water bombers to control fires if an earthquake interrupted the normal water supply. Vancouver recently installed an earthquake-resistant saltwater distribution system in its downtown core to fight fires. Modern construction methods and zoning regulations have reduced the potential for widespread fire damage in the Pacific Northwest. However, our systems of natural gas distribution to homes and industry still leave our communities vulnerable to serious fires from a large earthquake. Fires caused by the 1995 Kobe earthquake burned many blocks of the city and were responsible for the majority of the nearly 6000 fatalities. More localized fires also occurred during the 1989 Loma Prieta and 1994 Northridge earthquakes in California.

Flooding

Strong earthquakes can also cause flooding. Ground shaking and liquefaction may break underground water transmission lines, flooding streets and properties near the ruptures. A more serious scenario is the failure of a hydroelectric or water storage dam. During the 1971 San Fernando (Los Angeles) earthquake, the dam impounding Van Norman Reservoir came within a whisker of catastrophically failing. If it had failed, a deluge of floodwater would have overrun communities in the San Fernando Valley. Part of the earth-filled dam slumped into the reservoir. Its crest was lowered 9 metres, leaving less than 3 metres of freeboard and a narrow strip of earth holding in the reservoir. Many dams in the Pacific Northwest have been seismically upgraded since their construction, including all hydroelectric dams in southwestern British Columbia. Other dams in the region, however, might not withstand the very strong shaking of a nearby earthquake of magnitude 7 or larger. An example is the clay-cored earth-fill dam that impounds Sooke Lake, Victoria's source of fresh water. The dam could be damaged by a large earthquake on the Leech River fault, which extends beneath the structure.

Flooding could also affect low-lying areas bordering many rivers in the Pacific Northwest, including, for example, the Fraser, Squamish, Skagit, and Willamette rivers. Homes and businesses on floodplains are protected by **dykes**, which are flat-topped ridges constructed close to the river's edge to keep the river in its channel during floods. Most of the dykes are constructed of loose fill that might liquefy during an earthquake. Were this to happen, the dykes could sag or collapse, allowing river water to pour onto the floodplain. This hazard is a seasonal one, as flooding could only occur during times of high river flow – late spring and early summer in the case of the Fraser River, and spring, early summer, or fall for other rivers in the region. The flow of the Columbia River is so highly regulated by its many dams that flooding due to dyke failure is unlikely.

Sea dykes at the front of the Fraser River delta are likewise vulnerable to failure during a strong local earthquake. Much of Richmond, a city with 200,000 residents situated on the Fraser delta, lies below mean sea level and would be inundated at high tide were it not for the sea dykes that protect it.

Water contamination

Drinking and waste water treatment facilities can be damaged during an earthquake. If not treated, municipal water might be unsafe to drink, a problem that can be circumvented if residents boil their drinking water. But this may not be possible if electricity and gas supplies are interrupted after an earthquake, as is often the case. People may plan for such an eventuality by keeping a stockpile of bottled water for emergency use. Untreated sewage can foul rivers, the sea, and the coast after an earthquake, increasing the possibility of spread of some diseases.

Reprinted with permission of Graham Harrop.

Beware of Me
Tsunamis

The sea, washing the equator and the poles, offers its perilous aid, and the power and empire that follow it . . . "Beware of me," it says, "but if you can hold me, I am the key to all the lands.
— Ralph Waldo Emerson, *The Conduct of Life* (1860)

A POPULAR WINTER LEISURE ACTIVITY is to travel to the west coast of Vancouver Island or the ocean beaches of Oregon and Washington and witness the full fury of a Pacific storm. Waves, metres high, rush ashore in turbulent fury, driven by storm-force winds streaming off the ocean – an exhilarating display of the power of nature, made especially enjoyable from the comfort of a seaside bar!

Yet, these waves pale in comparison to a different type of ocean wave – tsunami! "Tsunami" is a Japanese word meaning "harbour wave." A commonly used term is "tidal wave," but that is a misnomer because these waves have nothing to do with tides. Rather, they are triggered by cataclysmic events – mainly large earthquakes beneath the ocean floor, although they can also be caused by landslides, volcanic eruptions, and even meteorite impacts.

A large tsunami can surge several kilometres inland and reach heights of 30 metres or more, smashing everything in its path. It may surprise you that tsunamis are imperceptible in the deep open ocean. Passengers on a ship crossing a tsunami would not even know they had done so. In the deep ocean, tsunami waves, travelling at speeds of many hundreds of kilometres per hour, have

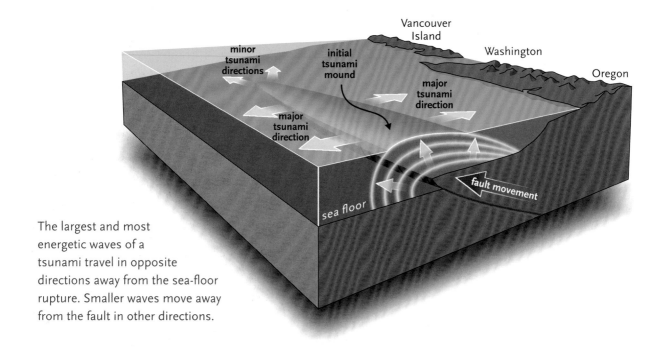

The largest and most energetic waves of a tsunami travel in opposite directions away from the sea-floor rupture. Smaller waves move away from the fault in other directions.

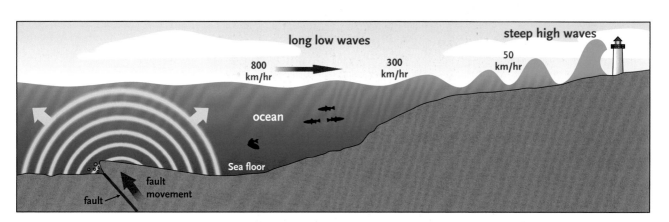

Simplified diagram showing a tsunami triggered by rupture of the seafloor along a fault during an earthquake. The sudden upward displacement of the sea floor initiates waves of energy that move upward and outward from the source. As the waves shoal, they slow down, move closer together, and become higher. They then transform into turbulent, landward-surging masses of water than may run kilometres inland.

heights of less than one metre and are separated from one another by kilometres. However, that changes as the waves approach shallow water near a coast. As the water shoals, the waves begin to decelerate, become more closely spaced, and grow taller. They eventually break and surge ashore with unimaginable force.

Before

The Scotch Cap lighthouse on Unimak Island, Alaska, was destroyed by a large tsunami triggered by a magnitude 8 earthquake on April 1, 1946. The five-storey lighthouse was nearly 10 m above sea level, but only its foundation and part of the concrete sea wall were left after the tsunami. Its five occupants were killed. The tsunami deposited debris up to 35 metres above sea level. Although little damage occurred elsewhere in Alaska, this tsunami was one of the most destructive ever on the Hawaiian Islands.

After

limit of tsunami damage zone

destroyed lighthouse

The catastrophic South Asia tsunami of December 2004

At 7:58 AM (local time) on December 26, 2004, the fault separating the India and Burma plates ruptured over a distance of 1200 kilometres along the Sundra Trench west of Thailand and Indonesia. The fault movement produced a magnitude 9.3 earthquake, the largest on Earth since 1960. It triggered a tsunami that claimed more than 200,000 lives in eleven countries bordering the Indian Ocean, including Somalia and Tanzania, 5000 kilometres from the epicentre. The only natural disasters to have claimed more lives in the last hundred years are a flood in China in 1938 and an earthquake in the same country in 1976.

The tsunami moved away from the epicentre at a velocity of about 700 kilometres per hour. Most of the wave energy was directed west and east, perpendicular to the fault line. Within minutes, the first tsunami waves swept across the coastal plain of

northwestern Sumatra to elevations up to 30 m above sea level, completely destroying scores of coastal towns. The provincial capital city of Banda Aceh was severely damaged by both the earthquake and the tsunami. The eastward-moving waves slowed as they crossed the shallow continental shelf west of Thailand and thus did not reach the tourist resorts of that country until about 10 AM, two hours after the earthquake. Shortly thereafter, waves up to four metres high surged ashore on the east coast of Sri Lanka and then southern India, wreaking widespread damage and claiming tens of thousands of

Computer simulation of the tsunami triggered by the giant Sumatra earthquake of December 26, 2004. The image shows the tsunami approaching Sri Lanka about two hours after the earthquake. Wave crests and troughs are shown, respectively, in red and blue. The colour intensity is a measure of the height of the wave or depression of the trough.

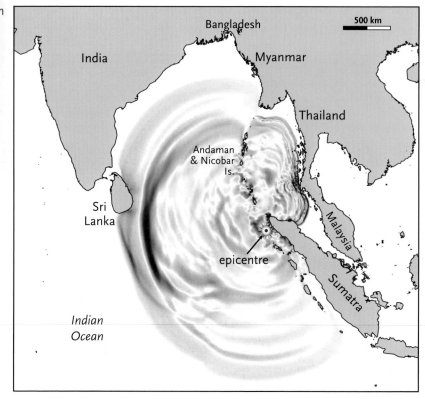

lives. Waves up to 4 metres high struck the Horn of Africa eight hours after the quake, killing about 150 people. Fortunately, the heavily populated southern part of Bangladesh, which lies just above sea level, was north of the main path of the tsunami, and the loss of life there was small. The tsunami eventually entered the Pacific Ocean and was even recorded at tidal stations on the west coast of Vancouver Island where its wave height was about 10 centimetres.

Even a rudimentary warning system might have saved tens of thousands of lives in South Asia. The tsunami struck Sri Lanka and India more than two hours after the earthquake, yet the people of these countries received no warning. Warning systems, however, are useful only when the source of the tsunami is far from populated shores. A warning system might not have helped the people of western Sumatra, where the tsunami arrived with full force less than 30 minutes after the earthquake. Furthermore, warning systems require a communications infrastructure that permits information to rapidly reach emergency officials in areas at risk. Those officials, in turn, should have plans to rapidly evacuate people from low-lying coastal areas.

Although it had horrific consequences, the Southeast Asia tsunami is not unprecedented. Tsunamis in the Pacific Ocean triggered by earthquakes in Chile in 1960 and Alaska in 1964 were just as large as the waves in the Indian Ocean, albeit nowhere near as lethal. The situation in the Pacific Northwest, however, is different from that in South Asia. First, we have had, since 1964, a tsunami warning system in the North Pacific, centred in Honolulu. Second, the total population in the Pacific Northwest at risk from tsunamis is, at most, some tens of thousands, much smaller than the millions who are threatened in Indonesia, India, and Sri Lanka. Third, large areas bordering the Indian Ocean are broad, low-lying coastal plains less than 10 metres above sea level and thus within the run-up zone of large tsunamis. Much of the outer Pacific coast, especially in British Columbia and Washington, is higher and steeper than in the Indian Ocean, which would limit the landward extent of tsunami damage. Fourth, the tidal range in the Indian Ocean is small and large numbers of people live at the edge of the sea in highly vulnerable positions. In contrast, on the Pacific coast, homes and buildings are set back from the upper limit of tides. Finally, most structures in which people live and work along the coasts of the Indian Ocean are flimsy and are no match for a tsunami. Debris entrained by the tsunami as it destroys these structures is just as lethal as the surging water itself. Although homes and other buildings in tsunami inundation zones on the Pacific coast would also be damaged and destroyed, better construction and materials ensure that this problem is not as severe.

Even without a warning system, however, the death toll in South Asia could have been much lower if people had responded to Nature's two tsunami warning signs. First, the strong ground shaking close to the epicentre, for example, in Banda Aceh and on the Nicobar Islands, warned of the likelihood of an approaching tsunami, giving residents in those areas many minutes to move inland or to higher ground. Second, at many distant locations where people would not have felt shaking, the first wave was preceded by a rapid withdrawal of the sea to levels that coastal residents would never normally see, a sure sign that a giant wave would soon strike the shore.

Satellite images of part of Banda Aceh in northwestern Sumatra taken six months before (top) and two days after (bottom) the December 26, 2004, tsunami. Nearly all of the buildings in this area were destroyed.

A popular misconception, reinforced by the Hollywood disaster movie *Deep Impact,* is that a tsunami consists of a single immense wave that curls over and crashes on the shore. A tsunami, however, is not a single breaker, but rather a series of waves separated by minutes to more than an hour. Generally, the second or third wave is the largest of the wave train, and in many instances the first wave is preceded by a recession of the sea. Rather than being curling breakers, the waves are typically turbulent, onrushing surges of debris-laden water. When one wave overtakes another, however, a steep wall of water, or **bore**, may be created.

Famous woodblock print of waves off the coast of Kanagawa, Japan by Hokusai Katsushika (1760–1849). For many people, the scene has become synonymous with tsunami, but it depicts storm waves; few tsunamis "break" in this manner.

Three sequential photographs show the arrival of a tsunami at Laie Point on the island of Oahu, Hawaii, on March 9, 1957. The tsunami was triggered by a magnitude 8.6 earthquake centred just south of the Aleutian Islands, about 3600 kilometres from Oahu. Blue arrows indicate the direction of the onrushing waters.

Tsunami sources

Earthquakes in the Pacific are the main sources of tsunamis on our coast. The quakes occur along subduction faults that cut the ocean floor off Kamchatka, Japan, Indonesia, the Philippines, and the west coasts of North and South America. When one of these faults suddenly slips during a great earthquake, a vast tract of ocean floor, up to 100 kilometres wide and hundreds of kilometres long, moves upward, displacing the water above it like a gargantuan piston. Waves move outward from the fault, travelling in stealth-like fashion hundreds of kilometres per hour toward the surrounding coasts.

Countries in coastal Asia have suffered the brunt of tsunamis in the historical period, but British Columbia and Washington are no strangers to these powerful waves. The most destructive historical tsunami in this area was triggered by the great Alaska earthquake of March 27, 1964. The tsunami moved outward from the epicentre of the earthquake near the head of Prince William Sound and, within a few hours, reached the Queen Charlotte Islands and Vancouver Island, damaging the communities of Port Alberni, Hot Springs Cove, and Zeballos. Although there was no loss of life in British Columbia, most of the 130 deaths caused by the "Good Friday" earthquake, including 16 in California and Oregon, were the result of tsunamis.

Tsunamis generated by distant earthquakes with epicentres thousands of kilometres from the west coast of North America pose a hazard to coastal communities in the Pacific Northwest. The worst-case scenario, however, lies at our doorstep – the great megathrust fault separating the North America and Juan de Fuca plates. When this fault next slips, as it last did in January 1700, the Pacific coast from Vancouver Island to northern California will be struck by tsunami waves far larger than those of March 1964. Computer simulations of such tsunamis (page 139) provide rough estimates of the size of waves than can be expected at different locations on the Pacific coast. For example, a

The tsunami generated by the 1964 Alaska earthquake moved rapidly across the Pacific Ocean from its source. The lines show the positions of the leading wave of the tsunami during the earthquake (time 0) and 8 minutes, 1 hour, and 4 hours later.

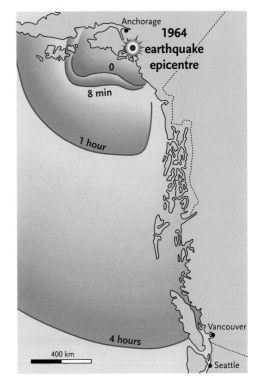

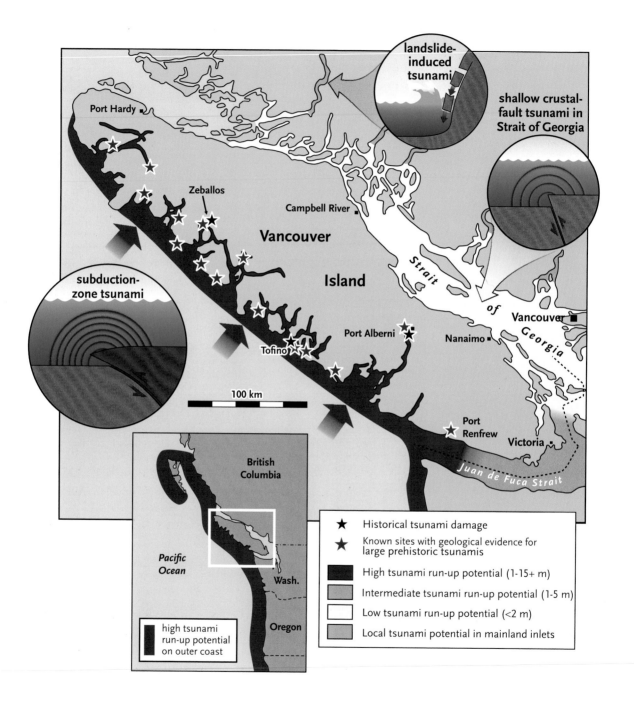

landslide-induced tsunami

shallow crustal-fault tsunami in Strait of Georgia

Port Hardy

Zeballos

Campbell River

Vancouver

subduction-zone tsunami

Island

Strait

of

Georgia

Port Alberni

Vancouver

Tofino

Nanaimo

100 km

Port Renfrew

Victoria

Juan de Fuca Strait

British Columbia

Pacific Ocean

Wash.

Oregon

high tsunami run-up potential on outer coast

★ Historical tsunami damage

★ Known sites with geological evidence for large prehistoric tsunamis

High tsunami run-up potential (1-15+ m)

Intermediate tsunami run-up potential (1-5 m)

Low tsunami run-up potential (<2 m)

Local tsunami potential in mainland inlets

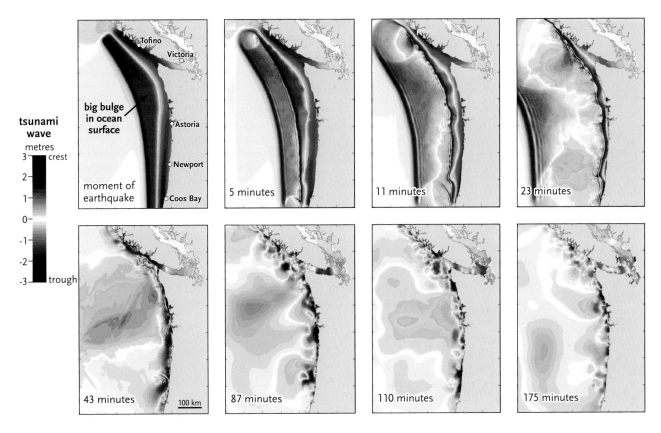

Computer simulation of a hypothetical tsunami triggered by a great earthquake at the north end of the Cascadia subduction zone. The eight panels show the progression of the tsunami eastward along Juan de Fuca Strait and into the Strait of Georgia and northern Puget Sound over a period of three hours following the earthquake. Compression of the high end of the colour range gives a misleading impression of wave heights along the outer coasts of Vancouver Island, Washington, and Oregon, where the tsunami first comes ashore. Waves at some sites on the outer coast may reach heights of 10 to 15 metres.

OPPOSITE

Tsunami hazard zones in coastal areas of southwestern British Columbia. Western Vancouver Island is at risk from large tsunamis triggered by great subduction earthquakes beneath the Pacific Ocean. The tsunami risk in the Strait of Georgia is much lower and is related to crustal earthquakes and undersea landslides. Local landslide-triggered tsunamis pose a hazard to some coastal communities, especially those at the heads of fjords.

simulated magnitude 8.5 earthquake at the northern end of the Cascadia subduction zone off Vancouver Island produces waves up to about 5 metres high on the west coast of the island. The waves amplify, however, as they move up inlets, attaining heights of 10 to 15 metres at some sites. Much energy is lost as the tsunami passes through narrow passages connecting Juan de Fuca Strait and the Strait of Georgia, and wave heights are reduced to a few metres by the time the tsunami reaches Victoria, and to one metre or less at Vancouver and Seattle. Of course, the state of the tide at the time the tsunami reaches the shore will influence run-up and, thereby, damage.

The Strait of Georgia and Puget Sound are protected from North Pacific tsunamis by Vancouver Island and the Olympic Peninsula, but these areas are vulnerable to tsunamis from another source. A large earthquake on a fault beneath either of these waterways could trigger a damaging local tsunami. Even the June 1946 Vancouver Island earthquake (magnitude 7.3), with an epicentre on land, not in the Strait of Georgia, produced a small tsunami that was responsible for the only fatality of the quake. Recently, geological investigations in Puget Lowland have shown that several faults crossing Puget Sound are capable of large, tsunami-producing earthquakes. About 1000 years ago, an earthquake of at least magnitude 7 on the Seattle fault triggered a tsunami in Puget Sound that locally reached heights of several metres. Traces of many other tsunamis have been found in tidal marshes near Everett and on the Olympic Peninsula. If a tsunami like that in about AD 1000 were to occur today, it would severely damage much development along the shores of Puget Sound.

Landslides that plunge into the sea or that occur on the ocean floor can also produce tsunamis. One of the greatest hazards to people living along the steep fjord coast of Norway, for example, is landslide-generated tsunamis. The British Columbia coast north of the Vancouver metropolitan area is sparsely populated compared to Norway's coast, but the hazard is similar and the risk will increase as the population and development on our coast grows.

The hazard is illustrated by a little-known event at Kitimat in 1975. A large submarine landslide in Douglas Channel, just south of the town, produced waves up to 8 metres high that caused about $2 million damage (2006 dollars) to shore facilities. The 1964 Alaska earthquake triggered a large submarine slump near Valdez, Alaska, that produced a local tsunami. The tsunami destroyed waterfront facilities, much of the fishing fleet, and claimed 30 lives, nearly 25 percent of all the casualties of the earthquake. More recently, in November 1994, a submarine landslide at the head of Taiya Inlet, just outside Skagway, Alaska, triggered a local tsunami with waves up to 11 metres high at the shoreline. That tsunami killed one person and destroyed more than 300 metres of a cruise ship dock that was being constructed at the time. On the Atlantic side of North America, the 1929 Grand Banks earthquake triggered a huge submarine landslide that severed sea floor telecommunication cables far out into the Atlantic and, more importantly, produced a tsunami that inundated the eastern coast of Burin Peninsula in Newfoundland, killing 27 people and causing widespread damage in many towns.

The most spectacular landslide-triggered tsunami of the twentieth century occurred on July 10, 1958, at Lituya Bay, Alaska. A strong earthquake triggered a rockslide on a steep slope high above the head of the bay. The rockslide plunged into the bay and displaced a huge mass of seawater that raced up the opposite valley wall to an elevation of 525 metres, completely destroying the forest in its path. In four minutes, a 30-metre-high wave surged 11 kilometres to the mouth of the bay, where it swept away two fishing boats anchored just inside a low forested spit. Remarkably, the crew of one of the boats survived and told a harrowing tale of their boat being swept over the tops of trees, across the spit towards the open Pacific Ocean.

Geologists have suggested that even larger tsunamis that the 1958 Lituya Bay event have been caused by collapses of the flanks of volcanoes on Hawaii in the Pacific Ocean and the Canary Islands in the Atlantic Ocean. Massive hummocky landslide deposits have been mapped on the sea floor adjacent to the Hawaiian Islands; some of them extend up to many tens of kilometres from the shore. The deposits are probably products of the collapse of the flanks of Mauna Loa and Kohala, two of the large volcanoes on Hawaii.

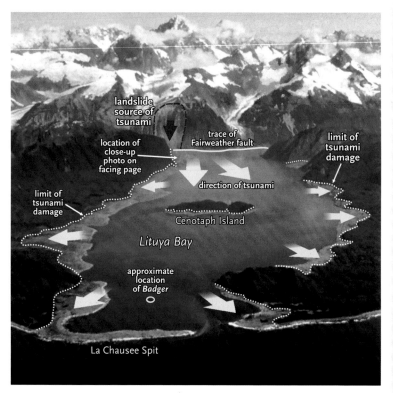

location of close-up photo on facing page

landslide source of tsunami

trace of Fairweather fault

direction of tsunami

limit of tsunami damage

limit of tsunami damage

Cenotaph Island

Lituya Bay

approximate location of *Badger*

La Chausee Spit

Lituya Bay shortly after the tsunami of July 7, 1958. The prominent trimline delineates the upper limit of the tsunami. Forests below this line were obliterated by the surging waters.

The 1958 Lituya Bay tsunami

Lituya Bay on Alaska's southeastern coast was the site of one of the largest tsunamis ever recorded. On the night of July 7, 1958, a magnitude 8.0 earthquake occurred along the Fairweather fault, which runs along the far northwestern part of the bay. The earthquake shook loose a large mass of rock high on the eastern wall of Gilbert Inlet at the head of the bay. The rock plunged into the inlet, triggering a tsunami of frightening proportion. Water surged more than 500 metres up the slope opposite the point of impact, stripping all vegetation and leaving a bare rock face. The wave swept westward to the head of the bay, inundating more than 10 square kilometres of land and clearing millions of trees. Unfortunate boaters who happened to be anchored near the head of the bay that night state that the wave was at least 30 metres tall there. Two of the boaters were killed by the wave while making a run for open water, but the rest, amazingly, survived.

Two of the survivors gave a graphic account of the event. Bill and Vivian Swanson entered Lituya Bay at about 9 PM on the night of July 7 and anchored their boat, the *Badger,* in about 7 metres of water inside La Chausee Spit, which separates the bay from the open Pacific Ocean. Mr. Swanson was wakened at 10:15 PM by violent vibrations of the boat caused by the earthquake. A little more than a minute later, but probably before the end of the earthquake,

Swanson looked toward the head of the bay, past the north end of Cenotaph Island and saw what he thought to be the Lituya Glacier, which had "risen in the air and moved forward so it was

in sight. . . ." After a little while, *"the glacier dropped back out of sight and there was a big wall of water going over the point"* (the spur southwest of Gilbert Inlet). Swanson next noticed the wave climb up on the south shore near Mudslide Creek. As the wave passed Cenotaph Island, it seemed to be about 50 feet high near the centre of the bay and to slope up toward the sides. It passed the island about 2½ minutes after it was first sighted, and reached the Badger about 1½ minutes later. No lowering or other disturbance of the water around the boat was noticed before the wave arrived. The Badger, still at anchor, was lifted up by the wave and carried across La Chaussee Spit, riding stern first just below the crest of the wave, like a surfboard. Swanson looked down on the trees growing on the spit, and believes that he was about 2 boat lengths (more than 80 feet) above their tops. The wave crest broke just outside the spit and the boat hit bottom and foundered some distance from the shore . . . Mr. and Mrs. Swanson abandoned their boat in a small skiff, and were picked up by another fishing boat about 2 hours later. [Don J. Miller, 1960, Giant Waves in Lituya Bay, Alaska; usgs Professional Paper 354-C.]

Other survivors reported that the wave crest seemed to be less than 15 metres wide, and that the back slope was less steep than the front. After the giant wave passed, the water surface was very turbulent, with much sloshing back and forth from shore to shore and with steep, sharp waves up to 6 metres high. These waves, however, did not show any definite movement either toward the head or the mouth of the bay. After 25 to 30 minutes, the bay became calm, although floating logs covered the water near the shores and were moving out toward the centre of the bay.

Rocky headland directly west of the landslide at the head of Lituya Bay. Water displaced by the landslide surged up this slope, removing the forest to more than 500 metres above sea level.

Geologists infer that these collapses triggered large tsunamis. In support of this idea, they note possible tsunami deposits on the slopes of Hawaii and Lanai, far from the present shore. The deposits contain fragments of coralline limestone, which otherwise occur only at and below sea level. The inference is that the fragments were deposited by waves up to several hundred metres high. If an event of this type were to occur today, parts of the Hawaiian Islands would be devastated. It is unlikely, however, that distant parts of the Pacific Rim would be affected in the same way. A tsunami generated by a landslide, even a very large one, attenuates significantly over distances of thousands of kilometres, and wave run-ups on the west coast of North America would not be catastrophic.

Let's turn our attention to the apocalyptic scenario so adored by Hollywood – a large meteorite or asteroid striking the North Pacific, as apparently happened in the Gulf of Mexico 65 million years ago, causing the extinction of the dinosaurs. If a meteorite one kilometre in diameter struck the Pacific Ocean, it might produce deep-water waves many tens of metres high that would run up some Pacific shorelines to elevations of more than 100 metres. Not a pretty picture for the hundreds of millions of people living along the coasts of the Pacific Ocean! Fortunately, the chance of such an event in our lifetimes is extremely low – lower than you, as one of 50 million ticket holders, might have of winning a lottery. Smaller meteorite impacts, however, are more likely than this, as are the smaller tsunamis they would trigger.

Damage in Hilo, Hawaii caused by the tsunami that resulted from the gigantic earthquake in Chile on May 22, 1960. The largest wave in Hilo was more than 10 metres high and traveled faster than 50 kilometres per hour. Note the scattered debris and the parking meters that were bent parallel to the ground by debris-laden surging water.

Tsunami damage

Most drowning caused by tsunamis happens when people are swept into deep water by the return flow. Floating debris is responsible for some of the deaths and much of the damage. Debris carried by tsunamis can generate very high impact forces. Floating wood pushed by tsunami bores, for example, may exert forces of many tonnes, which is greater than most structures can withstand. The return flow may also carry debris, with the same potential for injury and damage as an advancing tsunami bore. Tsunamis may also spread liquid contaminants, which is of concern in port areas where combustible materials such as fuel oil, gasoline, and other hazardous chemical compounds are common. In Japan, fishing vessels and other boats swept inland by tsunami waves have fueled fires sparked, for example, by overturned gas cooking appliances. Public health can also be compromised if a tsunami damages sewage and other wastewater services or water supply lines. Untreated wastewater may mix with the water supply, spreading infectious diseases.

The tremendous power of a tsunami is shown by a tire that was impaled by a 2 x 12 inch plank as waves rushed ashore in Whittier, Alaska, following the 1964 Alaska earthquake.

Banda Aceh, Indonesia, after the catastrophic tsunami of December 26, 2004. More than 200,000 people lost their lives during the tsunami.

Effects of the 1964 Alaska earthquake tsunami in the Pacific Northwest

The large tsunami, generated by more than 9 metres of seafloor uplift as a consequence of the 1964 Good Friday earthquake in Alaska, did considerable damage to coastal communities in the Pacific Northwest. Due to the southeasterly direction of seafloor thrusting, the tsunami's primary energy was focused onto the coast of North America and had lesser effects in Hawaii and Asia. The wave train, travelling at about 750 kilometres per hour, first struck the Queen Charlotte Islands where, at Shields Bay, the sea rose 5 metres above normal tidal level. When the tsunami reached Vancouver Island on the night of March 27, the tide was nearly high. Several small communities along the outer coast of the island, mostly located within or at the heads of inlets including Quatsino Sound, Kyoquot Sound, Nootka Sound, and Esperanza Inlet, were damaged. Many houses in the community of Zeballos at the head of Zeballos Inlet were flooded and some were dislodged from their footings. Charles Ford, a B.C. Airlines pilot living in Zeballos at the time, reported using his Winchester .308 to fire holes into the floor of his house to drain the water, further remarking "it wasn't much of a house anyway." Eighteen of the 20 houses at Hot Springs Cove were swept off their footings and carried inland. Some were swept into the inlet on the return flow.

The town of Port Alberni at the head of Alberni Inlet was extensively damaged. The inlet has a natural wave period that closely matched that of the tsunami waves, focusing and amplifying their energy. The lower parts of the city are near sea level and were the sites of small commercial businesses and residences adjacent to a large pulp mill, wet and dry log-sorting areas, and marinas. The first wave of the tsunami wave train was the smallest. It was followed by a second, much larger wave about an hour and a half later. Fortunately, the interval between the two waves was long enough to allow residents time to evacuate low-lying areas, which were then invaded by water carrying logs, boats, houses, and even cars. Shoreline businesses were extensively damaged, as were wharves, log booms, and submarine cables crossing the inlet. The

The 1964 tsunami at Port Alberni

The Alaska earthquake of March 27, 1964, triggered tsunamis that killed 130 people, some as far away as California. The main tsunami swept southward across the Pacific Ocean at a velocity of over 750 kilometres per hour (about 270 metres per second), reaching Port Alberni in six and one-half hours and Antarctica in only 16 hours. Waves grew in size as they moved up Alberni Inlet and were two and one-half times larger at Port Alberni at the head of the inlet than at Tofino and Ucluelet on the open coast.

Three main waves struck Port Alberni between 12:20 AM and 3:30 AM on March 28. Most people in the town were asleep when the first wave rolled in at or near high tide. The sea surged up Somass River at a velocity of about 50 kilometres per hour and spilled onto the land, inundating whole neighbourhoods in chest-deep water. This first wave peaked at 3.7 metres above mean sea level and knocked out the Port Alberni tide gauge.

The second and most destructive wave swept into town less than two hours later, at 2 AM. The lights of the waterfront mills went out as the water smashed

through the facilities. The ground floor of the Barclay Hotel, one kilometre inland, was splintered by the surging water; guests had to be plucked from an upper floor by police in boats. Logs and debris crashed into buildings, and houses were swept off their foundations and hurtled inland. As the water subsided, some buildings were dragged seaward; two houses drifted into Alberni Inlet and were never seen again. The second wave left a mark on the tide station at 4.3 metres above mean sea level.

The third wave, which arrived at about 3:30 AM, was the largest of all, but because the tide had fallen it crested at 3.9 metres and did little further damage. Other waves oscillated in Alberni Inlet for another two days with decreasing strength.

Two hundred and sixty homes in Port Alberni were damaged by this tsunami, and the total economic losses here and elsewhere on Vancouver Island were estimated at about $50 million (2006 dollars).

As destructive as it was, this event pales in comparison to some other historical tsunamis in the Pacific Ocean, notably the tsunami in the Indian Ocean in December 2004, which claimed nearly 300,000 lives. The eruption of Krakatoa in 1883 triggered a tsunami that killed about 37,000 people in Indonesia, and in 1896 waves up to seven stories tall struck the east coast of Japan, smashing more than 100,000 houses and drowning 26,000 people.

Damage in Aonae on Okushiri Island, Japan, caused by a tsunami on July 12, 1993. The tsunami was triggered by a magnitude 7.8 earthquake off the west coast of Hokkaido. The tsunami engulfed the coasts of Okushiri Island and adjacent Hokkaido. More than half of the two hundred fatalities associated with the earthquake were caused by the tsunami.

147

damage was estimated at $25 million (2006 dollars), but no lives were lost.

As the tsunami moved southward, it passed the entrance of Juan de Fuca Strait, paying little attention to the waters of the Strait of Georgia or Puget Sound. However, several people died along the coasts of Washington and Oregon, including four children in a single family. The small coastal town of Crescent City in northern California suffered the greatest damage. Twenty-nine blocks of the community and 150 businesses were destroyed. Many residents thought that the threat had passed when the first two, relatively small waves came ashore, and they returned to their homes or went down to the waterfront to survey damage done to businesses and boats. Forty minutes after the second wave arrived, the first of the giant waves, 4½ metres high, struck the community. It was followed by a fourth wave, over 6 metres high, some twenty five minutes later. These waves tore through the town, destroying everything in their path. Eleven people needlessly died because no evacuation orders were issued by the authorities, who were completely unprepared for the third and fourth waves.

Tsunami preparedness and warning

Tsunamis cannot be prevented, but the damage they cause can be greatly reduced through a variety of actions. These actions include land-use controls (zoning, relocation, and property acquisition), emergency preparedness, dyking, barrier construction, flood proofing, tsunami-resistant construction, warning systems, and public education. Public safety may require that certain uses of land in high-hazard areas be restricted through zoning regulations or by relocating structures to higher ground. However, these types of actions tend to be strongly resisted by residents who would be affected by them, as has been the case, for example, in Port Alberni.

Risk to coastal communities can be assessed by estimating the frequency and size of tsunamis from historical records and geological data. Computer-generated numerical models and the distribution of historic and prehistoric tsunami deposits give useful estimates of maximum tsunami heights expected along a given stretch of coastline. Maps can then be made showing areas likely to be inundated by tsunamis of different sizes. Such maps may help guide or restrict development in tsunami-prone areas and educate people living in these areas about the risks they face. Computer models also provide estimates of tsunami arrival times, currents, and forces on structures.

Properly constructed dykes and walls can stop waves from reaching threatened residential and commercial areas, but they are expensive and should be built to the highest possible elevation that can be reached by a tsunami. In some cases, offshore barriers can deflect tsunami waves or lessen their energy before they reach the shore. Again, these are expensive structures and may provide only limited protection. They are economically feasible only where large populations are at risk and where the threatened shoreline is at the head of a bay or inlet.

In areas of high tsunami hazard, buildings can be designed or protected to reduce water damage. Elevation of buildings and other types of flood proofing (for example, installation of seals for basement windows, bolting houses to their foundations) provide protection where water depths are not expected to exceed one metre and currents are not strong. Structures can be raised to higher levels to provide greater protection, but costs may be prohibitive. Some houses near the shoreline on the Hawaiian Islands, for example, have been built on piers, their floors elevated several metres above ground level to allow water to move freely beneath them.

Protection of life also requires effective tsunami warning systems. Such systems, however, are useful only when the tsunami originates far from populated shores. The travel times of tsunamis produced by earthquakes off Japan, Kamchatka, and Alaska are sufficiently long that low-lying coastal areas of British Columbia, Washington, and Oregon can be evacuated following alerts. When the source of the tsunami is less than about 100 kilometres away, there usually is insufficient time to warn and safely evacuate people, and no warning is possible when a local landslide triggers a tsunami. The shaking caused by a local strong earthquake, however, is a good warning of a possible tsunami.

Three types of warning systems exist for tsunamis in the Pacific Ocean: a Pacific-wide system (the Pacific Tsunami Warning Center) in Hawaii; regional systems, including the West Coast and Alaska Tsunami Warning System in Alaska; and local systems in Chile and Japan. The three systems rely on rapid estimates of earthquake magnitude and location to trigger warnings, followed by reports from coastal tidal stations to verify that a tsunami was produced. False alarms are common because not all large earthquakes trigger tsunamis and because most warnings are based on earthquake data, rather than direct tsunami observations. The governments of Alaska, Washington, Oregon, California, and British Columbia continue to work closely with the West Coast and Alaska Tsunami Warning Center to improve tsunami response in the North Pacific.

In recent years, interest has increased in using sea-floor sensors to record the passage of tsunamis in deep water. The U.S. National Oceanographic and Atmospheric Association (NOAA) has developed a network of deep-ocean reporting stations that can track tsunamis and report them in real time, a project known as Deep-Ocean Assessment and Reporting of Tsunamis (DART). The network includes sensitive ocean-bottom sensors that detect the passage of the tsunami over them. The sensors transmit pressure measurements to a buoy at the ocean surface, which then relays the information to a ground station via

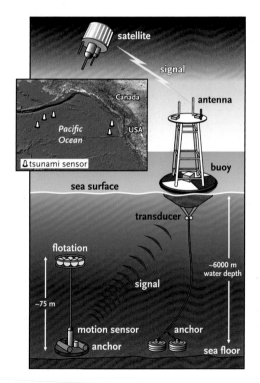

The Deep Ocean Assessment and Reporting of Tsunamis (DART) Project is an ongoing effort by NOAA to detect and report tsunamis in the open ocean. DART stations are located in regions with a history of destructive tsunamis to ensure early detection and to acquire data essential for real-time forecasts. The 6-buoy operational array shown in this figure was completed in 2001. A DART system consists of an anchored seafloor bottom pressure recorder, which can detect tsunamis as small as 1 cm in height on the open ocean, and a companion moored surface buoy for real-time data communication. The data are relayed via a satellite link from the buoy to ground stations, where they are processed and disseminated to NOAA's Tsunami Warning Centers.

satellite. The Neptune Project (see page 77), which is currently in the implementation stage, also will use sea-floor pressure sensors to detect tsunamis.

Even the most reliable tsunami warning system is ineffective if people do not respond in orderly and intelligent ways. Because tsunamis are infrequent, people's recollections, as with any rare natural phenomenon, fade with time. This can lead communities into a false sense of security, as happened, for example, at Crescent City. Education is therefore essential if communities are to become more resilient to tsunamis.

A public education program should provide tsunami information at regular intervals, perhaps annually, and should include instructions on how to get information during an alert, where to go, and what things to take. Educational initiatives should be included in school curricula to ensure that younger generations understand the hazards and potential impacts of tsunamis. Education about tsunamis should not be limited only to those living on or near the coast but to all communities, because people from inland regions often travel to tsunami-prone areas.

A range of educational initiatives can be undertaken in coastal

Many low-lying coastal communities, such as Manzanita, Oregon, are at risk from tsunamis. Residents in Oregon and Washington have been educated about the dangers. For example, warning signs alert visitors to the risk of tsunamis in these regions. British Columbia does not yet have a comparable educational program.

communities. Activity sheets containing graphics, pictures, data, questions, and other relevant information can be used in schools to educate students about tsunami hazards. Tsunami evacuation routes can be publicized and marked by signs, as has been done in Japan, the United States, and New Zealand. Citizens should be consulted about land use in the tsunami inundation zone before decisions are made about where to build critical facilities such as hospitals and police stations, high-occupancy buildings such as schools, and petroleum-storage tank farms. Tsunami information can be printed in newspapers and telephone books, along with phone numbers of local emergency service offices. All telephone directories in British Columbia coastal communities, for example, contain information on earthquakes and tsunamis. Citizens should also be regularly informed about local warning systems.

The Seventh Angel: Predicting Armageddon
Earthquake prediction

And there was a great earthquake, such as was not since men were upon the earth, so mighty an earthquake, and so great.
— The Revelation of St. John, The Divine 16, 18.

WHEN A SEISMOLOGIST gives a public lecture, the first questions often asked are "When will you be able to predict earthquakes?" and "When will the next one happen?" Scientists now can say generally where large earthquakes will occur and how frequent and large they are likely to be, but neither they nor publicity-seeking seers and crackpots are able to reliably say when. Earthquake prediction has enjoyed limited success in China (probably more by good luck than anything), and large sums of money have been spent on the effort there and elsewhere. However, the earthquakes that destroyed much of Kobe, Japan in 1995 and Bam, Iran in 2003 were not predicted, even though both cities lie within known earthquake-prone areas. Likewise, the catastrophic earthquakes in Chile (1960), Alaska (1964), Mexico City (1985), Armenia (1988), Turkey (1999), and Pakistan (2002 and 2005) were not predicted.

Our ability to forecast and ultimately predict earthquakes depends partly on how well we monitor the build-up of strain energy in the Earth and how long we have done this. In the Pacific Northwest, we have been

The 1975 Haicheng earthquake

On February 4, 1975, Haicheng, a city with about 100,000 inhabitants in Liaoning Province, northeast China, was struck by a magnitude 7 earthquake. As early as 1970, the State Seismological Bureau, had identified the area as having a high earthquake risk. It issued a prediction in June 1974 that a magnitude 5 to 6 shock might occur in the region in the next 1 to 2 years. This forecast was followed by a prediction on January 13, 1975, that there would be a magnitude 5.5 to 6 quake in the Yingkou-Dairen-Tantung region of Liaoning Province in the first six months of 1975. The State Seismological Bureau issued an imminent earthquake warning to the provincial and local Party and Revolutionary Committees on February 4, the day the quake struck. These warnings were based, in part, on precursor events and unusual animal behaviour. The ground was usually warm in the months preceding the earthquake. Ice melted on a frozen reservoir, and snakes left the earth and froze on the ground. As early as December 1974, observers noted that rats appeared as if drunk, chickens refused to enter their coops, and geese frequently took to flight. They also noted unusual sulphurous gas emissions in the Haicheng area. Two hours before the quake, water erupted from springs to heights of more than 2 metres. Very bright, red flashes glittered in the dark sky immediately before the shaking starting.

When the earthquake struck, there was little loss of life because most inhabitants had heeded the warnings and evacuated to safer places. But property damage was high. Ninety percent of the structures in the city were destroyed or severely damaged. Most of the inhabitants of Haicheng would have been killed had the earthquake not been predicted accurately enough to effect a massive evacuation of the local population on the afternoon and evening of February 4.

This event, however, stands in stark contrast to the great earthquake that struck the city of Tangshan in northern China without warning a little over one year later, on July 28, 1976. Tangshan, a thriving industrial city with one million inhabitants, is located 150 kilometres east, and slightly south, of Beijing. In the early morning hours of July 28, while the city's residents slept, a magnitude 7.5 earthquake ruptured an 8-kilometre section of a fault beneath the city. The devastation of the city was nearly total. Bridges, railroads, homes, and factories were completely leveled. The shaking was so strong that people were thrown into the air. The extent of the destruction and number of deaths in Tangshan was never disclosed officially. However, based on the density of population, it can be fairly accurately estimated that at least 250,000 people died, and a larger number were injured. Observers had noted no strange animal behaviour or precursor events, thus the earthquake struck without warning.

recording earthquakes for only about a century, and only during the last two decades have the recording instruments been sophisticated. This period is substantially shorter than in Japan and China, where documented observations and accounts of earthquakes extend back centuries.

Earthquake prediction

Two approaches have been used to try to anticipate future earthquakes. One is called "prediction" and the other "forecasting." A prediction specifies that an earthquake of a given magnitude will occur in a defined region within a restricted period of time (hours, days, weeks). Predictions are based on measurable changes, such as the frequency and strength of **foreshocks**, strain in surface and near-surface rocks, water levels in wells, and magnetic, electrical, and acoustic properties of the crust. Increases in the amount of naturally occurring **radon** in well water and peculiarities in animal behaviour have been thought to presage some earthquakes. Observers in earthquake-prone districts in China report odd animal behaviour to state officials. Reported behaviour includes, for example, the sudden emergence of large numbers of snakes or rats from the ground, flocks of birds suddenly taking flight, and agitation among domesticated animals. It seems likely that some animals can detect subtle changes in the Earth, perhaps in its magnetic field, that humans cannot sense. However, animals may behave strangely for many reasons, few of them having anything to do with earthquakes. It thus is unlikely that odd animal behaviour will ever be used to reliably predict earthquakes.

A significant dilemma in making a prediction is that it must be reliable; there is no room for error. If the prediction does not come to fruition, people will lose confidence in the predictor, a classic example of the "cry wolf" phenomenon. We are probably at least decades away from predictions that approach 100% accuracy. Thus, any prediction of the location, time, and magnitude of an earthquake should be accompanied by an estimate of the probability that it will happen.

"Seismo-seers" like to claim that they were correct in predicting that an earthquake would occur on southern Vancouver Island or in Puget Sound in such-and-such a week of a given year. But those regions sustain many earthquakes of low to moderate magnitude throughout the year, thus the prediction has a good statistical chance of being correct, although not useful. Similarly, some seers like to brag that they had predicted a large earthquake somewhere in the circum-Pacific region or in the mountainous areas of Europe or Asia in a particular year. Again, they would likely have been correct anyway because very large earthquakes occur in these regions at a rate of about one per year. A testable, useful prediction is one that gives a *time,* within a span of several days, a *location,* within a certain number of square kilometres, a *magnitude,* and a believable *scientific rationale.* For several years, the United States Geological Survey operated a recording telephone service for people wishing to make earthquake predictions. None of the recorded predictions met these criteria. Predictions based on the arrangement of planets in the solar system, the appearance of comets and meteor showers, peculiar weather, unexplained changes in the functioning of mechanical or electrical devices such as clocks and TV sets, or the sudden appearance of corns on Aunt Masie's left foot should not be taken seriously.

Earthquake prediction vs. forecasting

A large earthquake was successfully predicted at Haicheng in China following a lengthy period of foreshocks in late 1974 and early 1975. On the evening of February 4, 1975, a magnitude 7 quake caused much damage to houses and buildings at Haicheng, but the loss of life was greatly reduced because most people and their animals moved outside. However, some seventeen months later, at Tangshan, a large industrial city about 300 kilometres to the southwest, a magnitude 7.5 earthquake struck without any warning, killing over 250,000 people in less than six minutes.

The town of Parkfield on the San Andreas fault in California had sustained large (roughly magnitude 6) earthquakes about every twenty years from 1857 to 1966, gaining the dubious title of California's earthquake capital. On the basis of this history, the U.S. Geological Survey in 1984 forecast that a large quake would strike the Parkfield area sometime between 1987 and 1993. In 1985, it initiated a long-term earthquake monitoring project, termed the Parkfield Experiment, to better understand what happens on the San Andreas fault before, during, and after an earthquake. The experiment involves more than 100 researchers from the USGS, universities, and government laboratories. The scientists installed a dense network of instruments to capture the anticipated earthquake and reveal the quake process in unprecedented detail. And then they waited. The time of the forecast proved to be incorrect, although finally, on September 28, 2004, a magnitude 6 quake struck close to the town. During the time of the experiment, much larger, unanticipated earthquakes occurred on the San Andreas fault at Loma Prieta (1989) and Landers (1992). These quakes may have temporarily reduced the stress on the Parkfield portion of the fault.

Earthquake forecasting

A forecast is more general than a prediction. It specifies an increased statistical probability that an earthquake within a certain range of magnitude will happen in a region over a period of months, or even years. The trend today is to issue forecasts, because reliable predictions are not possible.

There are two types of earthquake forecasts: deterministic and probabilistic. Deterministic forecasts provide estimates of the largest earthquakes that a region or fault will experience within the next few decades. They can be made for crustal faults such as, for example, the Portland Hills, Seattle, and Devils Mountain faults (see pages 101 to 109). For each of these faults, the maximum moment magnitude of the largest earthquake associated with the structure is estimated by multiplying the area of the fault surface that is likely to rupture by the expected amount of slip on the fault, and then multiplying that product by the shear strength of the rocks involved. The maximum moment magnitude for these faults, all of which show evidence of slip in the past 10,000 years, is of the order 7.0 to 7.5. Faults that probably have not slipped for hundreds of thousands or millions of years are not considered seismic risks.

Probabilistic earthquake forecasts can be made when the history of slip events is known. Faults that have not slipped in millions of years have a very low probability of generating an earthquake in the foreseeable future. Probabilities are highest for faults that have had recurrent, recent earthquakes. To construct a

Earthquake prediction

Map showing seismic gap along the Queen Charlotte fault. The red dots show epicentres of historical earthquakes; the red squiggly lines indicate the rupture extents of large earthquakes in 1929, 1949, 1970, and 1972.

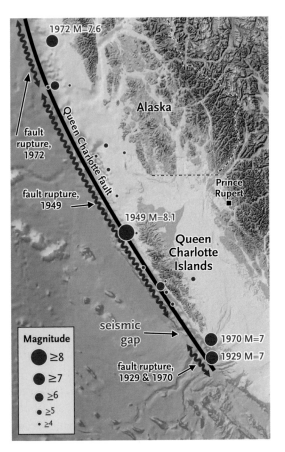

Seismic gaps

A potentially important indicator of future earthquakes along faults is what is termed a **seismic gap**. Portions of long faults that mark plate boundaries, such as the San Andreas fault in California, the Anatolian fault in Turkey, and the Queen Charlotte fault off the west coast of the Queen Charlotte Islands, have had no earthquakes for long periods of time, even though other parts of the faults have recently been active. It is reasonable to assume that all parts of these faults are active and will ultimately slip. Zones that have been seismically quiet in the recent past therefore may be more likely to experience an earthquake than those that have produced quakes recently. Some seismic gaps, notably those along the Anatolian fault, have produced devastating earthquakes in the last few decades, but many have not. Moreover, some parts of seismically active faults have produced several large quakes within short time intervals. There are no earthquake data in the Pacific Northwest to support or deny the presence of seismic gaps along the megathrust separating the Juan de Fuca and North America plates. Thus, apart from the Queen Charlotte fault, seismic gap theory has little application to the Pacific Northwest.

probability curve for an earthquake of a specific size on a particular fault we must know (1) the time the fault last slipped and (2) the average recurrence interval of earthquakes of the same size. The vertical axis of the diagram shows the probability, or likelihood, of the earthquake and ranges from zero to 100%. The horizontal axis records time. Immediately after an earthquake, the probability of another earthquake of similar magnitude is small. The probability of the next earthquake increases with the passage of time, reaching 50% at its average return period. It continues to increase beyond the average return period, although at a decreasing rate until it approaches 100%, or certainty of occurrence.

We have no record of earthquakes on known crustal faults in

157

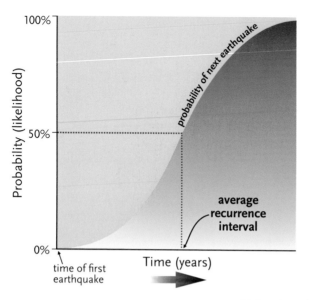

Probability (likelihood)

probability of next earthquake

average recurrence interval

time of first earthquake

Time (years)

Hypothetical probability curve showing the likelihood that an earthquake of a given magnitude will recur. Immediately after an earthquake, the probability of a second event of similar magnitude is near zero. As time progresses, the probability of the second earthquake increases. The average recurrence time is reached at a probability of 50%. After this, the probability continues to increase towards 100%, or certainty, of occurrence.

the Pacific Northwest in the historic period, so we don't know the times of the last earthquakes, nor do we know the recurrence interval of the earthquakes along them. Thus, the best we can do for these faults is make a deterministic forecast. In contrast, the earthquake history of many faults in California is sufficiently well known that the U.S. Geological Survey issues real-time forecasts of earthquakes in the state, as well as long-term probability forecasts of motion on individual faults in the San Francisco area.

Stephane Mazzotti and John Adams have suggested that the Pacific Northwest may still be within the shadow of the AD 1700 event and that this effect will disappear in about 100 years, leaving the region open to another megathrust quake. Some seismologists think that the earthquake will have a magnitude of about 8 and will rupture only part of the subduction zone fault, whereas others think that its magnitude will be 9 or more and that it will rupture the entire 1000 kilometre length of the fault.

The last seven subduction earthquakes in the Pacific Northwest seem to have occurred in two clusters (page 86). Coastal geological data show that three great earthquakes happened between about 3500 and 2400 years ago, and three more occurred between about 1700 and 1000 years ago. The two clusters were separated by at least 700 years. The last event of the younger cluster was followed by a quiet period of 700 years, prior to the most recent quake in AD 1700. The coastal geological data thus hint at the possibility that the 1700 event marks the beginning of a new cluster of earthquakes.

Stephane Mazzotti (Geological Survey of Canada).

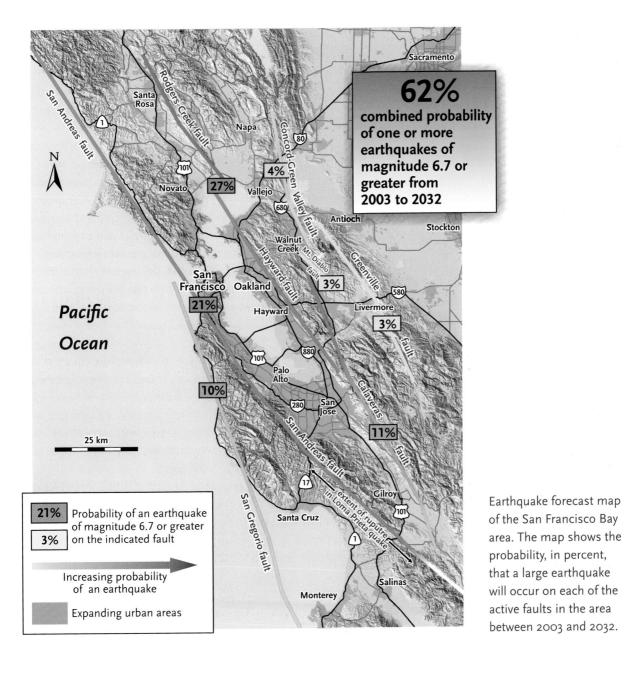

62% combined probability of one or more earthquakes of magnitude 6.7 or greater from 2003 to 2032

San Andreas fault

Rodgers Creek fault

Santa Rosa

Napa

Concord-Green Valley fault

Sacramento

Novato

Vallejo

4%

27%

Antioch

Stockton

Walnut Creek

Mt. Diablo fault

Greenville fault

Hayward fault

San Francisco

Oakland

3%

Hayward

Livermore

21%

3%

Pacific Ocean

Palo Alto

Calaveras fault

San Jose

10%

11%

San Andreas fault

extent of ruputre in Loma Prieta quake

Gilroy

San Gregorio fault

Santa Cruz

Salinas

Monterey

N

25 km

21% / **3%** Probability of an earthquake of magnitude 6.7 or greater on the indicated fault

Increasing probability of an earthquake

Expanding urban areas

Earthquake forecast map of the San Francisco Bay area. The map shows the probability, in percent, that a large earthquake will occur on each of the active faults in the area between 2003 and 2032.

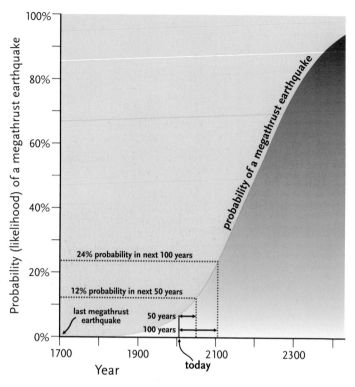

The growing likelihood that a great Cascadia subduction earthquake will occur over time since the last such quake in AD 1700.

Mazzotti and Adams postulated that earthquakes within clusters occur, on average, every 355 years and that clusters are separated, on average, by 840 years. Assuming the 1700 event was the beginning of a short interval cluster, they calculated an earthquake recurrence probability of about 30% in the next 50 years. If, on the other hand, one assumes there is no clustering, the probability (0% at 1700) rises with time and reaches 12% 50 years from now, and 24% 100 years from now.

A curve showing the probability over time of a great subduction earthquake in Cascadia, based on Mazzotti's and Adams' analysis and assuming a non-clustering scenario, is shown on the left. The curve shows there is a 50% chance that the next great quake will occur within 500 years of the last such event (AD 1700), or sometime in the next 200 years. A similar approach can be used to estimate the probability of earthquake shaking at any particular level of intensity at different places in the Pacific Northwest.

The transient slow-slip events described on page 76 have implications for earthquake forecasting in Cascadia. Modelling of precisely known surface location data indicates that each of the slow slip events involves about 30 millimetres of movement along the fault down-dip of its locked portion, with a total energy release equivalent to a magnitude 6.6 to 6.9 earthquake. This amount of slip accommodates about two-thirds of the long-term convergence of 4 centimetres per year between the Juan de Fuca and North America plates. According to Mazzotti and Adams:

> … *the recently discovered deep slow-slip events on the Cascadia subduction zone dramatically modulate the probability of a great subduction earthquake. During the*

two-week slow-slip events, the weekly probability of a great earthquake is about 30 to 100 times as high as at other times. A slow-slip episode might be predicted months ahead based on past periodicity and its commencement can be confirmed from a combination of GPS and episodic tremor evidence about 48 hours after it has begun. The prediction would allow an immediate pre-event campaign of public earthquake awareness. Rapid confirmation of a slow-slip event could allow emergency measures organizations to implement selected disaster mitigation activities during the remainder of the event duration.

If seismologists can one day identify the specific slow-slip event that triggers a megathrust earthquake, we might have at least a few days to get ready for it.

The most useful data for generating a forecast in the Pacific Northwest may be detailed measurements of crustal strain accumulating in surface rocks. Such measurements have been made through repeated geodetic surveys and, recently, continuous tracking of points on the Earth's surface with satellite-based global positioning systems (GPS). Sophisticated GPS systems can measure vertical and horizontal changes in points on the Earth's surface within a few

The probability that a damaging earthquake (Mercalli Intensity VII) will occur within 100 years for various cities and towns in British Columbia.

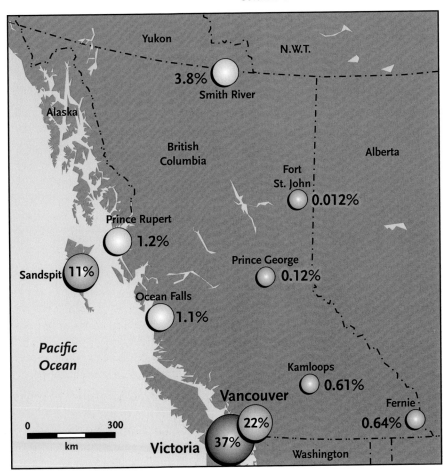

millimetres. So far, these surveys have only been done on land, but in the near future, the joint U.S.-Canada Neptune Project will offer GPS data across the boundary separating the Juan de Fuca and North America plates on the Pacific Ocean floor. Although the Neptune Project will not in itself allow scientists to predict earthquakes, it will no doubt improve earthquake forecasting.

A special aspect of forecasting involves estimating the intensity of the largest earthquake that can occur within a region. Estimates of the strength and duration of ground shaking that can be expected are extremely important for determining where to build public infrastructure such as dams, nuclear power plants, hospitals, schools, and stadiums. Strong motion seismographs placed in regions of frequent earthquakes can provide data for estimating intensities and assigning a degree of **seismic risk**.

An important product of earthquake forecasting is the application of seismic risk analysis to national building codes. The Geological Surveys of Canada and the U.S. Geological Survey have issued maps showing anticipated peak horizontal ground accelerations that have a one-in-ten chance (10% probability) of occurring within the next 50 years (page 46). This scheme for expressing earthquake probability may seem obscure, but it is useful to engineers who are charged with designing public buildings and other large structures.

Other maps can show how incoming seismic waves affect or are modified by rocks or sediments through which they pass. The figure opposite shows differences in ground motion that are expected for a moderate-sized earthquake in Victoria. Loose sediments overlying bedrock would amplify low-frequency seismic waves. The amount of amplification depends on the thickness and composition of the sediments. Further amplification can occur from the focussing of energy in areas where sediments thin against rising bedrock slopes. Surface bedrock produces little or no amplification. The map also shows areas that might suffer other earthquake effects, including liquefaction and landslides. Similar kinds of maps have been made for communities in Oregon and California, and an earthquake hazard map is being developed for Seattle.

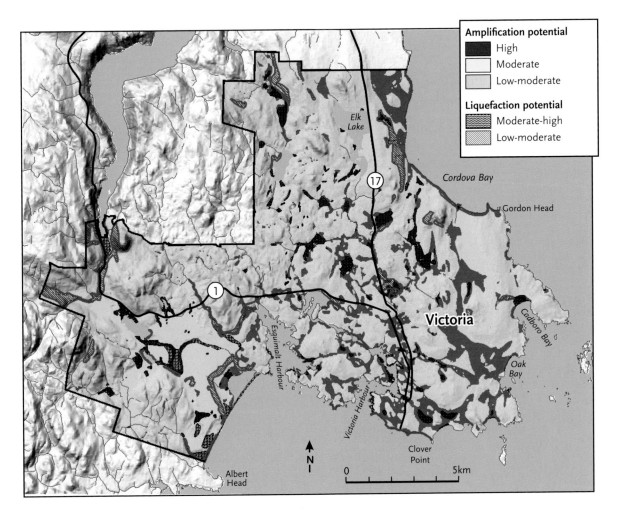

Earthquake hazard map of the Greater Victoria area. The map shows the influence of different soil types on ground shaking, as well as areas where liquefaction can be expected during a moderate to strong earthquake. Areas of thick sediment and fill that can significantly amplify ground shaking are shown in red.

What value are earthquake forecasts?

Because large earthquakes in the Pacific Northwest cannot reliably be predicted, it is not clear what governments should do to alleviate their effects other than to enforce appropriate building codes and upgrade public infrastructure that is likely to be damaged. The fact that a large quake is certain to happen in the next 500 years is unlikely to interest politicians whose attention span rarely extends beyond the next election. The current mayors of many coastal communities are not going to lose sleep over today's forecasts of earthquakes hundreds of years into the future, nor can they be expected to. After all, this is not California, where large earthquakes are more common near densely populated areas than in Cascadia and can be expected to occur within the lifetimes of civic and state officials.

The potential social and economic consequences of earthquake prediction and forecasting deserve careful consideration. A reliable prediction of a potentially damaging earthquake a year in advance may substantially reduce casualties and even property damage, but the social and economic disruption may be considerable. Property values could decline, together with tax revenues. Insurance and mortgage funds might become much less available. Business activity and opportunities for employment might decline. If the prediction was shorter-term, say only a day, panic might render transportation systems useless, resulting in greatly increased casualties. Even if continuing research eventually provides short-term predictions as accurate as weather forecasts, the uncertainty will still be great enough to put seismologists into the awkward position of being damned if they do make an accurate prediction and equally damned if they do not.

The Readiness Is All
Preparing for earthquakes

If it be now, 'tis not to come; if it be not to come, it will be now; if it be not now, yet it well come: the readiness is all....
— William Shakespeare, *Hamlet*, Act 5, Scene 2

Earthquake preparedness is the responsibility of individuals, groups, and governments. An informed and prepared populace will result in greatly reduced injury and death when a large quake occurs. In this chapter, we provide some basic information on how to prepare for an earthquake and what to do during and after the quake. This information has been culled from literature provided by Public Safety and Emergency Preparedness Canada (PSEPC), the British Columbia Emergency Preparedness Program, and the Insurance Bureau of Canada. Our treatment of the subject is necessarily brief because the focus of our book is earthquake science. For other sources of information see "Want More Information" on page 173.

Informative brochures on how to prepare for an earthquake are available from various organizations and government agencies.

165

Before the shaking starts

Most earthquake casualties result from partial building collapse and falling objects such as chimneys and light fixtures. Consequently, it is important to know the safe spots in each room of your house or apartment. Safe spots include inside walls, supported archways, and the undersides of sturdy tables and desks. Danger spots include windows, fireplaces, and areas adjacent to heavy hanging objects and tall unsecured furniture. Do not rush outside during an earthquake, as debris from the outside of the building and power lines may fall to the ground.

Families should discuss and prepare an emergency plan. Start by discussing what you should do at home, at school, or at work if an earthquake strikes. Prepare a list of what needs to be done ahead of time to be prepared. Divide up the task so that everyone involved participates as much as possible. Write down and exercise your plan, and make sure everyone in the family has a copy. If you live alone, develop a plan for yourself with links to neighbours and friends. Pre-select an appropriate out-of-the-area contact that should be notified about the family's status after the earthquake. This contact, ideally a family member or close family friend, can pass on news to other family members if individuals are separated. Learn first aid and CPR, and keep a list of emergency telephone numbers. Ask for the emergency plan for your children's school. Know the safe places to be, and where not to be, in your home during an earthquake.

You can take simple, inexpensive measures to prepare your home for a quake:

Falling objects are responsible for much of the injury and death caused by earthquakes. This building in Coalinga, California, was destroyed by an earthquake in May 1983. Most of the brick exterior of the building collapsed, but the wood-frame interior is largely intact.

- Learn how to shut off your gas, water, and electricity. Clearly label the on-off position for the gas, water, and electricity.
- Make sure your house is bolted to its foundation.
- Repair loose roof shingles.
- Make sure chimneys are strong and well braced.
- Keep breakable and heavy objects on bottom shelves of cabinets.
- Secure heavy furniture that could topple, such as bookcases, cabinets, and wall units.
- Strap water heaters to walls.
- Secure appliances that could move enough to rupture gas or electricity lines.
- Do not place heavy pictures and other items over beds.
- Position beds and chairs away from chimneys and windows.
- Put secure latches on cabinet doors to prevent dishes and glassware from spilling out.
- Put anti-skid pads under televisions, VCRs, computers, and small appliances, or secure them with Velcro or other such products.
- Keep flammable and other hazardous liquids such as propane cylinders, solvents, and paints in the garage or in a shed away from the house.
- Check chimneys, roofs, walls, and foundations for structural damage.
- Put plywood up in the attic on joists around each chimney to prevent masonry from coming through the ceiling.
- Maintain a supply of emergency food, water, and other supplies in a secure, easily accessible area. These should include a flash-light, candles, waterproof matches, fire extinguisher, duct tape, pen, note pad, wrench, pocket knife, manual can-opener, whistle, battery-powered radio, extra batteries, essential medication, personal toiletry items, money, first aid kit, temporary shelter (a plastic tarpaulin or small tent), and clothing. Your food and water should be sufficient to last for three to five days. Choose foods that require no refrigeration, cooking, or preparation, and are compact and lightweight.
- Store an emergency kit in your car, tool shed, or garage in case you have to evacuate your home and can't go back in.

During the shaking

The best advice during an earthquake is "don't panic." If you are indoors, stay there. Move away from windows, glass partitions, mirrors, fireplaces, bookcases, tall furniture, and light fixtures. Do not get underneath the grand piano because the heavy metal sounding board may collapse on you. Get under a desk or table, or place yourself in an archway or inside corner of a room. Once there, protect your head and face. Avoid doorways, as doors may slam shut and cause injury. Do not use an elevator or run from the building. If you are in an elevator, get out as soon as you can. If you are outdoors, move to an open area away from buildings, windows, trees, and power lines. If driving, pull over to the side of the road away from power lines, bridges, overpasses, and buildings. Stay in your vehicle until the shaking stops. If you are in a crowded public place, try to take cover where you won't get trampled. Do not run for exits; sidewalks next to tall buildings are particularly dangerous because of falling glass and other materials. Keep away from windows, skylights, and display shelves laden with heavy objects.

When the shaking stops

Try to remain calm. Check yourself and others nearby for injuries. Administer first aid, but do not move seriously injured individuals unless their life is in immediate danger. Place a HELP sign in your window if you need assistance. Put on sturdy shoes and protective clothing to prevent injury from debris and hunt for hazards:

- Fires, gas and water leaks, arcing electrical wires, and broken sewage lines. If you suspect damage, turn the utility off at the source. However, do not turn off gas if there is no damage.
- If you smell gas, extinguish all fires, do not use matches, and do not operate electrical switches. Open windows, shut off the gas valve, leave the building, and, if possible, report the leak to authorities.
- Check your home for damage, including the roof, chimney, and foundation.

The next step is to check and secure your food and water supplies. If tap water is available, fill a bathtub or other containers. Emergency water may also be obtained from water heaters, melted ice cubes, and toilet tanks. Purify water by boiling it for several minutes. If you have lost your power, strain the water through paper towels or several layers of clean cloth. Clean up any spilled hazardous materials, wearing proper hand and eye protection. Do not use barbecues, camp stoves, or unvented heaters indoors. Do not flush toilets if the sewage line is damaged.

Do not use the telephone unless there is a severe injury or fire; chances are that phones will not work anyway. Emergency phone numbers are found on the inside cover of most telephone books. Do not use your vehicle unless there is an emergency; it is important to keep streets clear for emergency vehicles. Do not leave your car if downed power lines are across it. Avoid waterfront areas in case of a tsunami. If you have pets, try to find and comfort them and keep them where you can find them in case you have to evacuate. Turn on your portable radio or television for instructions and news reports. Rely on emergency authorities for guidance. Be prepared for aftershocks.

For more information on earthquake preparedness, you may wish to contact:

- Geological Survey of Canada, Pacific Geoscience Centre
- U.S. Federal Emergency Management Agency (FEMA)
- United States Geological Survey
- Emergency Services Division, Health Canada
- Canada Mortgage and Housing Corporation (CMHC), Canada's housing agency
- The British Columbia Provincial Emergency Program (PEP)
- The British Columbia regional office of Public Safety and Emergency Preparedness Canada in Victoria (PSEPC)
- Oregon Office of Emergency Management
- Washington State Emergency Management Office

The responsibilities of governments

Governments must do their share in preparing for earthquakes. An individual could possibly be excused for taking no action, given the low probability of being injured in a quake, but federal, provincial, state, and local governments do not have this luxury. Their cities will, without doubt, be there when the next large quake strikes, and governments have the primary responsibility for earthquake-proofing critical infrastructure.

Our governments have responded on this issue, although some would argue that the resources they allocate for earthquake preparation are too few and the pace of activity too slow. The Canadian and U.S. governments have seismic provisions in their building codes that ensure that public buildings and other critical infrastructure are built to withstand the shaking of moderate to large earthquakes. Provincial and state governments have seismically retrofitted formerly vulnerable highway bridges and tunnels, and

The Lions Gate Bridge in Vancouver is one of the many bridges in the Pacific Northwest that have been upgraded to better withstand earthquake shaking.

utilities have strengthened dams in earthquake-prone areas. The British Columbia Government recently committed funds to accelerate retrofitting of old schools in the Victoria and Vancouver areas, largely in response to citizen pressure.

Could governments do more? Yes. They could provide financial incentives to their citizens to make their homes more resistant to earthquakes. The governments of British Columbia, Washington, and Oregon could assist their outer coastal communities to prepare for tsunamis. They could also allocate more money to speed up retrofitting of older, more vulnerable infrastructure. Provincial and state governments could also strengthen earthquake and tsunami education in schools and better educate the general populace on these phenomena. Finally, they and the federal governments could provide additional resources for disaster response. The poor response of the U.S., Louisiana, and Mississippi governments following Hurricane Katrina vividly shows that much needs to be done by governments in preparing for inevitable natural disasters.

The Scarfe (Education) building on the campus of the University of British Columbia, an example of a seismically retrofitted structure. A network of external, diagonal iron beams protects the building from failure during a strong earthquake.

What is the current state of our earthquake preparedness in the Pacific Northwest? Because we have not experienced a great, destructive earthquake, many have a somewhat casual attitude toward the threat. Seismic retrofitting of public buildings and schools is slowly progressing, but insurance and liability issues place obstacles on private and public earthquake mitigation initiatives. We can gain some sense of the danger from Alaskans' experience with the giant 1964 earthquake. Forty years after that event, however, you would not see much evidence that Anchorage's population remembers what happened. Much of the devastated area of Turnagain Heights has been turned into a park. But large housing developments have appeared on the flanks of the slide, and the Fourth Avenue slide area is unrecognizable. In only four decades, the greatest recorded earthquake to strike North America is regarded as little more than a hiccup in the history of the city.

Of what use is this faded memory to the people of Cascadia? The 1964 Alaska earthquake provides the best example of what we can expect in the Pacific Northwest during the next great earthquake at the Cascadia subduction zone. But it provides little of value for dealing with the several minutes of strong shaking that the earthquake unleashes, the period during which most of the destruction and loss of life will occur. Following the earthquake, several emergency measures organizations will respond at different rates and effectiveness to carry out the functions they learned during countless make-believe training and study sessions. Helicopters carrying sombre politicians will survey the scene, and premiers, governors, prime ministers, and presidents will promise relief that they may not be able to deliver. In the last analysis, when the shaking stops and the tsunami has ebbed, it will be Cascadia's people who cope with the disaster and begin to rebuild the Pacific Northwest. Then, they will peacefully sleep, at least until it happens again.

Want More Information?

MORE THAN ONE HUNDRED books have been written on earthquakes. Those listed below are a sample, a starting point if you are interested in learning more about earthquakes and related phenomena. The publications are divided into two groups – general books on earthquakes, some technical and others non-technical; and books, reports, maps and other papers on earthquakes and earthquake-related issues in British Columbia, Washington, Oregon, and California. The non-technical books are suitable for students and the general public; the technical publications require some knowledge of seismology, geophysics, or geology. Recommended Web sites follow the lists of publications.

General books

Bolt, Bruce A. 2003. *Earthquakes* Fifth edition. W.H. Freeman & Co., 320 p. [technical]
   This book provides a good overview of earthquakes, from how and why they happen to their effects and safety concerns. It includes information on faults, tectonic plates, earthquake magnitude, earthquake forecasting, ground acceleration, and soil conditions, among many other topics.

Brumbaugh, David S. 1998. *Earthquakes: science and society.* Prentice Hall, 251 p. [non-technical]
   This book covers the scientific, historical, and personal safety aspects of earthquakes. It provides the basic scientific facts

about earthquakes, explains how the science of seismology has progressed through time, gives details on the development of earthquake instruments, and considers practical aspects such as personal safety and building and living in areas prone to earthquakes.

Chambers, Catherine. 2001. *Earthquakes (Disasters in nature).* Heinemann Educational Books, 48 p. [non-technical]
   "Disasters in Nature" is a series of short books intended to educate readers about the effect of disasters on the environment, their human impact, and how we deal with them. Up-to-date research, case studies, stunning photography and explanatory diagrams help to illustrate the points.

Coburn, Andrew and Spence, Robin. 2002. *Earthquake protection.* Second edition. John Wiley & Sons, 436 p. [non-technical]
   A guide to environmental planning for earthquakes. The book discusses prediction and preparation, as well as emergency management and recovery. It examines earthquake protection strategies; considers site selection, seismic hazard assessment, and improving earthquake resistance of buildings; addresses loss estimation, and risk and vulnerability analysis; and assesses possibilities for reducing earthquake disasters. The book includes recommendations for further reading.

Dolgoff, Anatole. 1998. *Physical geology.* Hougton Mifflin, 638 p. [technical]
   An introductory earth science textbook with an excellent section on seismology. The book is well written and illustrated with colour photographs and drawings.

Hough, Susan E. 2002. *Earthshaking science: what we know, and don't know, about earthquakes.* Princeton University Press, 272 p. [non-technical]
   This book is an excellent summary of our current approaches to understanding earthquakes. It integrates state-of-the-art research with explanations of earthquake phenomena and attempts to explain many of the current controversies.

Levy, Matthys, Salvadori, Mario, and Lilly, Michael. 1995. *Why the Earth quakes: the story of earthquakes and volcanoes.* W.W. Norton & Company, 216 p. [non-technical]

> The authors use examples from history to explore how human-made structures fare in the wake of earthquakes and volcanic eruptions. They briefly explain the nature of the Earth, and then discuss modern engineering solutions for keeping buildings upright during earthquakes.

Lomnitz, Cinna. 1994. *Fundamentals of earthquake prediction.* John Wiley & Sons, 344 p. [non-technical]

> This book explores the history of earthquake prediction, methods, successes and failures, and new directions. Topics include earthquake prediction in China, monitoring ground-water, big quakes in Chile and Japan, plate tectonics, animal behaviour, aftershocks and precursors, risk analysis, disaster theory, how structures hold up (or don't), and earthquake prediction and politicians.

Morgan, Lael. 1993. *Earthquake survival manual.* Epicenter Press, 160 p. [non-technical]

> Tips for preparing for and surviving an earthquake.

Nance, John J. 1988. *On shaky ground.* William Morrow, 416 p. [non-technical]

> The author describes the great Alaska earthquake of 1964, and also gives information on the Mississippi Valley quake of 1811 and the Chile quake of 1960. He discusses the history of the science of seismology and its exponential growth in the twentieth century. But while demonstrating that seismology is becoming an exact science, he points out that the public is deaf to the warnings of experts, citing examples where people have rebuilt on ground that has been proven to be unsafe.

Prager, Ellen J. 1991. *Furious Earth: the science and nature of earthquakes, volcanoes, and tsunamis.* McGraw-Hill/Contemporary Books, 235 p. [non-technical]

> The author brings together top scientists to examine the

nature of earthquakes, volcanoes, and tsunamis. It provides the story and science behind these forces, from the Earth's evolution and plate tectonics to disaster warnings.

Ritchie, David and Gates, Alexander E. 1994. *The encyclopedia of earthquakes and volcanoes.* Checkmark Books, 306 p. [non-technical]

The 1000-plus alphabetical listings range from historical volcanoes and earthquakes to entries on specific seismic phenomena and general geological principles, including a few excellent in-depth discussions on topics like plate tectonics and seismic wave types. The encyclopedia also contains a lengthy bibliography, a list of internet resources, a chrono-logical listing of notable earthquakes and eruptions, and some eyewitness accounts.

Scholtz, Christopher H. 2002. *The mechanics of earthquakes and faulting.* Second edition. Cambridge University Press, 496 p. [technical]

The two major themes of this textbook are the connection between fault and earthquake mechanics, and the central role of the rate-state friction laws in earthquake mechanics. Chapters cover mechanics of faulting, mechanics of earth-quakes, the seismic cycle, seismotectonics, and earthquake prediction and hazard analysis.

Sieh, Kerry E. and LeVay, Simon. 1999. *The Earth in turmoil: Earthquakes, volcanoes, and their impact on humankind.* W.H. Freeman & Co., 324 p. [non-technical]

An account of what we now know about volcanoes and earth-quakes. It explores natural hazards in the U.S. region by region, combining accounts of past disasters with predictions for the future. The final chapter of the book describes how people can mitigate the damaging effects of earthquakes and volcanoes through individual and collective action.

Steinbrugge, Karl. 1982. *Earthquakes, volcanoes and tsunamis: an anatomy of hazards.* Skandia America Group, 392 p. [technical]

Although now more than two decades old, this book provides an excellent review of seismic and volcanic hazards. The book's perspective is global.

Wyss, Max and Dmowska, Renata (editors). 1997. *Earthquake prediction – State of the art.* Birkhauser, 264 p. [non-technical]
   The debate regarding our ability or inability to predict earthquakes is examined in this book. Proponents of prediction methods present their cases, whereas critics point out shortcomings. Included in this volume is a list of significant earthquake precursors that may be useful for prediction attempts.

Yeats, Robert S., Sieh, Kerry E., and Allen, Clarence R. 1997. *The geology of earthquakes.* Oxford University Press, 568 p. [non-technical]
   A readable primer on earthquakes by some of the world's foremost authorities on the subject.

Publications on the Pacific Northwest and California

Adams, J. and Atkinson, G. 2003. *Development of seismic hazard maps for the proposed 2005 edition of the National Building Code.* Canadian Journal of Civil Engineering, v. 30, p. 255–271. [technical]
   A technical paper describing how geophysicists prepared the earthquake hazard maps for the next iteration of the National Building Code of Canada

Adams, J. and Halchuk, S. 2003. *Fourth generation seismic hazard maps of Canada: values for over 650 Canadian localities intended for the 2005 National Building Code of Canada.* Geological Survey of Canada Open File 4459, 155 p. [technical]
   Summarizes the methods that were used to produce the new seismic hazard maps of Canada. The report includes expected earthquake ground motions for more than 650 localities that will be listed in the next National Building Code of Canada and also includes maps of seismic hazards for Canada.

Alt, David D. and Hyndman, Donald W. 1978. *Roadside geology of Oregon.* Mountain Press Publishing Co., 272 p. [non-technical]
An excellent layman's guide to the roadside geology of Oregon.

Alt, David D. and Hyndman, Donald W. 1984. *Roadside geology of Washington.* Mountain Press Publishing Co., 278 p. [non-technical]
An excellent layman's guide to the roadside geology of Washington.

Atwater, Brian F. and 15 others. 1995. *Summary of coastal geologic evidence for past great earthquakes at the Cascadia subduction zone.* Earthquake Spectra, v. 11, p. 1–18. [technical]
The geologic record of great (magnitude 8 to 9), subduction earthquakes in the coastal Pacific Northwest and its implications for seismic risk in the region.

Atwater, Brian F., Musumi-Rokkaku, Satoko, Satake, Kenji, Tsuji, Yoshinobu, Ueda, Kazue, and Yamaguchi, David K. 2005. *The orphan tsunami of 1700: Japanese clues to a parent earthquake in North America.* University of Washington Press; also U.S. Geological Survey Professional Paper 1707, 133 p. [non-technical]
This wonderful book tells the story of a mysterious tsunami that arrived in Japan one winter's night in January 1700 without the warning that a nearby earthquake provides. It recounts the scientific evidence from both sides of the Pacific that implicates a giant earthquake off the west coast of North America as the source of the tsunami.

Castell, Graem. 2002. *Earthquake! Preparing for the big one: British Columbia.* Pacific Rim Earthquake Preparedness Program Ltd., Vancouver, 292 p. [non-technical]
A comprehensive, well written book on earthquake preparedness. The book describes measures that can be taken to reduce the damage and possibility of injury during a strong earthquake.

Clague, John J. 1996. *Paleoseismology and seismic hazards, southwestern British Columbia.* Geological Survey of Canada Bulletin 494, 88 p. [technical]

A summary of the historic and prehistoric earthquake history of southwestern B.C. and northwestern Washington state. The report also includes a discussion of seismic hazards and risk in the region.

Clague, John J. 1997. *Evidence for large earthquakes at the Cascadia subduction zone.* Earthquake Spectra, v. 35, p. 439–460. [technical]

Review of the geological and geophysical evidence for great earthquakes in the coastal Pacific Northwest.

Clague, John J. 2002. *The earthquake threat in southwestern British Columbia: a geological perspective.* Natural Hazards, v. 26, p. 7–34. [technical]

A summary of the record of large historic earthquakes in the coastal Pacific Northwest and discussion of the likely impacts of a similar quake near a city in the region in the future.

Clague, John J., Luternauer, J.L., and Mosher, D.C. 1998. *Geology and natural hazards of the Fraser River delta, British Columbia.* Geological Survey of Canada Bulletin 525, 270 p. [technical]

A comprehensive overview of the geology of the Fraser River delta. It includes a chapter on earthquakes.

Clague, John J., Munro, A., and Murty, T. 2003. *Tsunami hazard and risk in Canada.* Natural Hazards, v. 28, p. 433–461. [technical]

History of tsunamis in Canada and a discussion of the likelihood and possible impacts of tsunamis in the future.

Cohen, Stan. 1999. *8.6: The great Alaska earthquake March 27, 1964.* McGraw-Hill, 235 p. [non-technical]

A well illustrated book, rich in anecdotes, that describes the Alaska earthquake of March 27. 1964. The "Good Friday" earthquake is the third largest seismic event in recorded history and is similar to great subduction earthquakes in the Pacific Northwest.

Fradkin, Philip L. 1998. *Magnitude 8: earthquakes and life along the San Andreas Fault.* University of California Press, 348 p. [non-technical]

A guide to the San Andreas fault and the large earthquakes that have occurred in California over the last 150 years. The author includes stories of legendary earthquakes elsewhere: in New York, New England, the central Mississippi River valley, Europe, and the Far East. He examines the mythology, culture, social implications, politics, and science of earthquakes.

Hyndman, R.D. 1995. *Giant earthquakes of the Pacific Northwest.* Scientific American, v. 273, no. 6 (June), p. 50–57. [technical]

An excellent summary of the development of the hypothesis that great earthquakes occur at the Cascadia subduction zone.

Jeffers, H. Paul. 2003. *Disaster by the Bay: the great San Francisco earthquake and fire of 1906.* The Lyons Press, 204 p. [non-technical]

Written by a veteran journalist and author and illustrated with many recently rediscovered photographs, this book tells the incredible story of the 1906 San Francisco earthquake and fire.

Mayse, S. 1992. *Earthquake: surviving the big one.* Lone Pine Publishing, 192 p. [non-technical]

This book describes how to prepare for an earthquake and what to do during and after one. Its geographic focus is south-coastal British Columbia, but residents of Washington and Oregon will find the book valuable.

Monger, J.W.H. (editor). 1994. *Geology and geological hazards of the Vancouver region, southwestern British Columbia.* Geological Survey of Canada Bulletin 481, 316 p. [technical]

A collection of papers on the bedrock and surficial geology, landslides, earthquakes, volcanic hazards, and groundwater in the British Columbia Lower Mainland.

Monger, Jim and Mathews, Bill. 2005. *Roadside geology of southern British Columbia.* Mountain Press Publishing Co., 404 p. [non-technical]

Authoritative and up-to-date guide to the southern third of British Columbia, including Vancouver Island.

Reisner, Marc 2003. *A dangerous place: California's unsettling fate.* Pantheon Books, 181 p. [non-technical]
A summary of California's rise from a largely deserted land to the most populous and economically important state in the U.S. Reisner focuses on the Los Angeles and San Francisco Bay areas, which are two of the most seismically active zones on Earth. The book concludes with a hypothetical but realistic description of a disastrous earthquake near San Francisco and its after affects.

Yeats, R.S. 2003. *Living with earthquakes in California: A survivor's guide.* Oregon State University Press, 416 p. [non-technical]
This how-to manual for life in earthquake country describes California's violent geologic past and recounts the state's efforts to grapple with the earthquake threat. It examines major faults that threaten California and Nevada, reviews the current level of earthquake preparedness and disaster response, and suggests actions that citizens can take to protect their families and homes. Topics discussed include earthquake forecasting, catastrophe insurance, and tsunamis.

Yeats, R.S. 2004. *Living with earthquakes in the Pacific Northwest: A survivor's guide.* Second edition. Oregon State University Press, 390 p. [non-technical]
A thorough treatment of the threat of a large-magnitude thrust earthquake on the Cascadia subduction zone and an extensive discussion of measures to prepare for and mitigate the expected damage.

Yorath, C.J. 1990. *Where terranes collide.* Orca Book Publishers, 231 p. [non-technical]
A readable book on the geologic evolution of the mountains of Western Canada and the geologists who work in this region. The book focuses on the assembly of crustal blocks, or

terranes, by plate convergence and subduction, which have created the present western margin of North America.

Yorath, C.J. 2005. *The geology of southern Vancouver Island.* Harbour Publishers, 205 p. [non-technical]
A description of the geological history and architecture of southern Vancouver. The second half of the book describes the geology of 26 field trip locations from Greater Victoria to Pacific Rim National Park.

Web sites

There is an enormous amount of material about earthquakes on the Internet. Some of this material is excellent; some is of dubious value; and some is just plain wrong. The following sites offer authoritative, up-to-date information and will lead you to other reliable sites.

http://www.pgc.nrcan.gc.ca/seismo/ – Geological Survey of Canada, National Earthquake Hazards Program, western Canada

http://neic.usgs.gov – U.S. National Earthquake Information Center

http://www.geophys.washington.edu/SEIS/ – University of Washington, Geophysics Program

http://www.geophys.washington.edu/tsunami/ – University of Washington, Geophysics Program

http://www.pmel.noaa.gov/tsunami/ – U.S. Department of Commerce, National Oceanographic and Atmospheric Association

http://cires.colorado.edu/people/jones.craig/EQimagemap/global.html – Web earthquakes

http://www.earthquakes.com/ – Global Earthquake Response Center

http://pasadena.wr.usgs.gov/step/ – U.S. Geological Survey, real-time forecast of earthquake hazard in California

Glossary

Accelerometer: A *seismometer* that measures the acceleration of the ground during an earthquake. It is designed for use in earthquake epicentral areas where the normal recording range of standard seismographs is exceeded.

Amplification (also called **seismic amplification**): The ratio of ground motion at a *sediment* site to that at a rock site. The amount of the amplification depends primarily on the physical properties and thickness of sediments through which the waves travel. The intensity of shaking can vary by a factor of three or more over small areas due to this effect.

Amplitude: The height of a wave (a seismic or earthquake wave in the context of this book).

Aseismic: Crustal deformation or slip along a *fault* that occurs without earthquakes.

Basalt: A black, fine-textured *igneous rock* containing minerals rich in iron, magnesium, and calcium. The upper part of oceanic *crust* consists of basalt.

Blanco fracture zone: The *transform fault* connecting *Gorda* and *Juan de Fuca Ridges.* See pages 26 and 30.

Body wave: A *seismic wave* that travels outward from an earthquake *focus* through the interior of the Earth.

Body wave magnitude: A measure of earthquake magnitude based on *primary waves.* It is used for earthquakes that are distant from recording stations.

Bore: A turbulent, wall-like water wave with a high, abrupt front, caused by a *tsunami,* the meeting of two tides, or a rapid rise in tide up a long narrow estuary, bay, or tidal river.

Carbon dating (**radiocarbon dating**): A method of determining the time of death of an animal or plant *fossil* by measuring the concentration of a radioactive *isotope* of carbon (carbon-14) in the fossil. Material that can be dated by the radiocarbon method includes wood, leaves, charcoal, shell, and bone. The method is limited to fossils that are less than about 50,000 years old.

Cascadia subduction zone: A zone about 1000 km long off the coasts of northern California, Oregon, Washington, and Vancouver Island, where the *Juan de Fuca plate* subducts beneath the *North America plate.* See pages 24, 26 75, 96, and 99.

Clastic dyke: An inclined tabular-shaped body of *sediment,* commonly silt or sand, that cuts across the natural horizontal or gently dipping layering of the host sediment. Many clastic dykes result from the upward flow of a slurry of water-saturated sediment derived from a liquefied layer at depth (see *liquefaction*).

Cocos plate: One of the *plates* forming the outer shell of the Earth, located beneath the Pacific Ocean off the coasts of Mexico and Central America. See page 63.

Compressional wave (also termed **P wave**): Seismic *body waves* that are transmitted by alternating compression and expansion in the direction of propagation. Like sound waves, they can travel through solids, liquids, and gases.

Continental shelf: A submerged platform that forms a fringe around a continent and extends to about 200 m depth. It lies just landward of the *continental slope* and is geologically part of the continent.

Continental slope: A pronounced submarine slope descending to the deep sea floor just beyond the seaward margin of the *continental shelf.*

Core: The innermost zone of the Earth, below about 2900 kilometres depth. The core is 3700 kilometres thick and lies below the *mantle.*

Coseismic: Abrupt crustal deformation or slip along a *fault* during an earthquake.

Crescent terrane: A large block of the Earth's *crust,* located on southern and western Vancouver Island, Washington, and Oregon, and consisting largely of oceanic volcanic rocks (see page 71 and 109). The Crescent terrane became attached to North America about 42 million years ago due to changes in the direction of movement of the *Farallon plate.*

Crust: The outermost layer of the Earth, composed of rocks rich in silicon and aluminum (granitic or continental crust) and silicon and magnesium (basaltic or oceanic crust). The crust ranges in thickness from 8 km beneath the oceans to more than 60 km beneath the continents.

Crustal earthquake: An earthquake that occurs on a *fault* within the *crust.*

Crustal plate: See *plate.*

Debris avalanche: A type of *landslide* in which a mass of *sediment* and vegetation rapidly slides down a slope.

Debris flow: A mass of water, clay- to boulder-size *sediment,* and plant debris that moves rapidly down a steep valley, gully, or ravine. Debris flows are commonly triggered by heavy rain.

Debris slide: See *debris avalanche.*

Delta: A low, nearly flat, triangular- or fan-shaped feature near the mouth of a stream or river. A delta is composed of *sediment* carried by a stream or river into the sea or a lake.

Diatoms: Microscopic unicellular or colonial algae with siliceous skeletons.

Dip-slip earthquake: An earthquake produced by a sudden upward or downward movement of rock along a dipping *fault*.

Dyke: An artificial wall or ridge built around a flat, low-lying area to protect it from flooding. Also used for a tabular body of *igneous rock* intruded into and at an angle to the layering of its host rocks.

Epicentre: The point on the Earth's surface that is directly above the *focus* of an earthquake,

Eurasia plate: One of the large *plates* that forms the outer shell of the Earth. It includes Europe, Asia, and adjacent seafloor areas. See pages 21 and 23.

Explorer plate: One of the *plates* forming the outer shell of the Earth, located north of the *Juan de Fuca plate* west of northern Vancouver Island (see pages 24 and 70). It is separated from the *Juan de Fuca plate* by the *Nootka fault*. The Explorer plate is breaking up and being consumed as the North America plate overrides it.

Explorer Ridge: The section of *mid-ocean ridge* separating the *Pacific* and *Explorer Plates*. See pages 26 and 30.

Farallon plate: A former large, oceanic *plate* located beneath the eastern North Pacific Ocean off the west coast of North America (see page 28). The *Juan de Fuca plate* is the last remnant of the Farallon plate.

Fault: A fracture within the Earth's crust along which rocks have moved past one another.

Feldspar: A family of minerals composed of silicon, oxygen, aluminum and one or more of the elements calcium, sodium, and potassium. The feldspars are the most abundant of all minerals in the *crust* and form by crystallization from molten *magma.*

Fjord (or **fiord**): A deep, long, narrow, steep-walled inlet or arm of the sea along a mountainous coast. A fjord is the submerged part of a glacially eroded valley. Local examples are Howe Sound and Alberni Inlet.

Floodplain: Flat, low land adjacent to a river channel. The floodplain is underlain by *sediments* deposited by the river when it overflows its banks.

Focal depth: The vertical distance from the *epicentre* of an earthquake to its *focus.*

Focus (also termed **hypocentre**; see also *epicentre*): The point within the Earth that an earthquake rupture starts and the source of its elastic waves.

Foreshock: An earthquake that precedes a large quake, commonly by minutes, hours, or days. It is smaller than the main earthquake that follows it.

Fossil: The naturally preserved remains or traces of an animal or plant.

Gas hydrate: A crystalline solid resembling ice. It consists of molecules of methane gas formed by decomposition of organic matter, each molecule surrounded by a cage of frozen water molecules. It is stable at ocean-floor temperatures and pressures and is most abundant within accreted sediments at subduction zones.

Gorda plate: One of the *plates* forming the outer shell of the Earth, located south of the *Juan*

de Fuca plate and between the *Pacific* and *North America* plates (see pages 30 and 77). The Gorda plate is being fragmented by a complex process involving subduction and stress related to plate motions along the San Andreas fault.

Gorda Ridge: The section of *mid-ocean ridge* separating the *Pacific* and *Gorda plates* (see page 30).

Hypocentre: See *focus*.

Ice Age: A period when climate was generally colder than today and ice sheets periodically covered large parts of northern North America, northern Europe, and Eurasia. The Ice Age spans the interval from about 2 million years ago until 10,000 years ago.

Igneous rock: Rock formed from molten or partly molten material.

In-slab earthquake: An earthquake with a *focus* within the *Juan de Fuca plate* below the *North America plate*.

Intensity: A measure of the effects of an earthquake on humans and structures at a particular place.

Isoseismal map: A map of an area affected by an earthquake showing lines of equal *intensity*.

Isotherm: A line of equal or constant temperature on a graph, plot, or map (see drawing on page 72).

Isotope: Any of two or more species of a chemical element having the same atomic number and position in the periodic table, but with different atomic mass. Oxygen, for example, occurs naturally as isotopes with atomic masses of 16, 17, and 18.

Juan de Fuca plate: One of the *plates* forming the outer shell of the Earth, located between the *Pacific* and *North America plates* west of northern California, Oregon, Washington, and Vancouver Island (see pages 21 and 24).

Juan de Fuca Ridge: The section of *mid-ocean ridge* separating the *Pacific* and *Juan de Fuca plates*. See pages 24 and 26.

Kula plate: A former crustal *plate* beneath the northeast Pacific Ocean off the west coast of North America (see page 28). The Kula plate was destroyed about 43 million years ago by *subduction* beneath the Aleutian trench.

Landslide: Any of a variety of downslope movements of rock, *sediment*, or a mixture of the two.

Lateral spread: The movement of a mass of rock or *sediment* along a horizontal or near-horizontal slip surface, accompanied by surface ground cracking and subsidence.

Liquefaction: The transformation of water-saturated granular *sediment* into a fluid by some external vibration force, commonly an earthquake.

Local magnitude: A measure of earthquake magnitude based on large-amplitude *shear waves*. It is used for earthquakes with epicentres close to recording stations.

Logarithm: An exponent representing how many times that a number (the base) has to be multiplied by itself to produce a given value. For example, the number 10, expressed to the base of ten, has a logarithm of 1; 100 (10 × 10) has a logarithm of 2.

Love wave: A seismic wave that travels at the

Earth's surface with motion transverse to the direction of propagation.

Magma: Molten rock within the Earth, from which *igneous rocks* form.

Magnitude: A numerical measure of the amount of energy released during an earthquake. Numerous scales and measures of magnitude have been devised for different purposes, including the *Richter scale* and modern *moment magnitude* scale.

Mantle: The zone in the Earth below the *crust* and above the *core*, extending from about 8–70 km to about 2900 km depth.

Megathrust earthquake: A large earthquake caused by the sudden slip of two plates at a subduction zone. Megathrust earthquakes occur at the *Cascadia subduction zone.*

Mid-ocean Ridge: A rugged ridge on the ocean floor with a central rift valley located along a zone of fractures into which new crustal material is injected from the underlying *mantle.*

Modified Mercalli Intensity Scale: An earthquake *intensity* scale, with 12 divisions ranging from I (not felt by people) to XII (damage nearly total).

Moment magnitude: A logarithmic measure of earthquake size, obtained by multiplying the rupture area of a fault by the amount of slip and the shear strength of the rocks.

Nazca plate: One of the *plates* forming the outer shell of the Earth, located off the west coast of South America between the *Pacific* and *South America plates.* See pages 21 and 23.

Nootka fault: The *fault* forming the boundary between the *Juan de Fuca plate* and the *Explorer plate* (see pages 30 and 70). It trends in an easterly direction from *Juan de Fuca Ridge*, a *spreading centre* in the eastern Pacific Ocean, to central Vancouver Island.

Normal fault: A generally steep fault along which the rocks above the fault have moved downward relative to rocks below the fault. It is generally the result of crustal tension or extension.

North America plate: One of the large *plates* that forms the outer shell of the Earth. It includes North America, part of Siberia, Greenland, and the western half of the Atlantic Ocean (see pages 21 and 23).

P wave: See *primary wave.*

Pacific plate: One of the large *plates* that forms the outer shell of the Earth. It includes much of the seafloor of the Pacific Ocean. See pages 21 and 23.

Pacific Rim terrane: A large block of the Earth's *crust*, located on western and southern Vancouver Island (see pages 71 and 109). It became attached to North America about 54 million years ago due to *subduction* of the *Kula plate* beneath the continent.

Pacific Ring of Fire: The zone of abundant earthquakes and active volcanoes that roughly follows the margin of the Pacific Ocean (see page 14). It marks boundaries between several large tectonic *plates.*

Paleozoic: An era of geologic time, extending from about 543 million to 248 million years ago.

Pangea: The name given to a supercontinent that

formed by collisions and amalgamation of most of Earth's continents during the late *Paleozoic.*

Period: The length of time separating successive seismic or other waves. Also a fundamental unit of geologic time.

Philippine Sea plate: One of the large *plates* that forms the shell of the Earth. It includes the seafloor south of Japan (see page 21).

Pillow basalt: A *basalt* with interlocking, pillow-shaped masses ranging from a few centimetres to a metre or more in diameter. Pillow basalts are formed when lava flows into a lake or the sea.

Plate (or **tectonic plate**): One of the large, nearly rigid fragments that form the *crust* and upper *mantle* of the Earth. Plates are 5 to 250 km thick.

Plate tectonics: A generally accepted theory based on the hypothesis that a small number (10 to 25) of crustal *plates* of different size "float" on the plastic upper *mantle* and move more or less independently of one another. Plates grind against each other like ice floes in a river. Much of the dynamic activity is concentrated at the periphery of plates, which are propelled from the rear by *seafloor spreading* and pulled from the front by *subduction.* Continents are part of plates and move with them, like logs frozen in ice floes.

Precambrian: The time from the birth of the Earth to the beginning of the *Paleozoic;* i.e., from about 4600 million to 543 million years ago. The Precambrian represents about 90% of geologic time.

Primary wave (also called **P wave**): A seismic wave that is propagated through the Earth by alternating compression and expansion of material in the direction of travel. See *compressional wave.*

Pyroxene: A group of dark-coloured, *igneous* silicate minerals composed of oxygen, silicon, calcium, magnesium, iron, and aluminum. Pyroxene is common in *basalt* and oceanic *crust.*

Quartz: A mineral compound of silica and oxygen, formed during crystallization of *magma* and a common constituent of continental *crust.*

Queen Charlotte fault: The fault marking the boundary between the *Pacific* and *North America plates* north of Vancouver Island (see pages 24, 99, and 157). It is a *transform fault* along which the two plates move mainly horizontally with respect to one another.

Radiocarbon dating: See *carbon dating.*

Radon: An invisible, odourless radioactive gas formed by the radioactive decay of radium, which is itself a decay product of uranium.

Rayleigh wave: A type of *seismic wave* that travels at the Earth's surface with a retrograde, elliptical motion.

Recurrence interval: The average time interval between natural events such as earthquakes or floods of a particular size.

Richter scale: The range of numerical values of earthquake magnitude, determined from trace deflections on a standard *seismograph* at a distance of 100 km from the *epicentre.*

The scale was developed by Kiyoo Wadati in 1931 and later modified by C.F. Richter. It is *logarithmic* – an increase of one in magnitude, for example from 3 to 4, corresponds to a ten-fold increase in the amplitude of ground motion and to approximately a 30-fold increase in energy. The threshold of significant earthquake damage is about magnitude 4 or 5. The largest earthquakes have magnitudes of about 9.5. See *moment magnitude*.

Rock avalanche: A type of *landslide* involving rapid streaming of blocky rock debris following the catastrophic failure of a cliff or steep slope.

Rockfall: A type of *landslide* involving the precipitous fall of a rock mass from a cliff or very steep slope. The rock mass breaks up into many blocks as it bounds down slope.

Rockslide: A type of *landslide* involving the sudden and rapid sliding of a rock mass on a slope. The rock mass generally breaks up into many blocks or fragments as it moves down slope.

S wave: See *shear wave*.

Sand blow: See *sand volcano*.

Sand volcano (also termed **sand blow**): A mound of sand produced by the upward movement and expulsion of sand-laden water through *sediments*. Sand volcanoes commonly form during earthquakes.

Seafloor spreading: The process whereby oceanic crust is produced by convective upwelling and cooling of magma along *mid-ocean ridges*. Newly formed oceanic crust moves away from the ridges at rates of 1 to 10 cm per year. See *plate tectonics*.

Sediment: Fragmented earth material that originates from weathering of rocks. Sediment is transported by, suspended in, or deposited from air, water, or ice. It may also form by chemical precipitation from solution. Sediment forms at the Earth's surface at atmospheric temperatures in a loose, unconsolidated form.

Sedimentary rock: Any rock formed by chemical precipitation or by deposition and cementation of mineral and rock grains that are carried to the site of deposition by water, wind, ice, or gravity.

Seiche: An oscillation of the surface of a lake, bay, or harbour that varies in period from a few minutes to several hours and in height from several centimetres to a few metres. Seiches can be triggered by local changes in atmospheric pressure aided by winds or tidal currents, and by earthquakes.

Seismic amplification: See *amplification*.

Seismic attenuation: A decrease in the severity, or *intensity*, of earthquake shaking due to a change in topography, or the character or thickness of the material through which seismic waves travel.

Seismic gap: A section of an active fault that has not been the source of a significant earthquake for a considerable time. It may have a greater probability of a large earthquake than adjacent sections that have ruptured more recently.

Seismic risk: The probability of injury, damage, or loss due to an earthquake.

Seismic wave: An elastic wave of energy generated by an impulse such as an earthquake, explosion, or meteor strike. Seismic waves travel through the Earth and are recorded by *seismographs*.

Seismic zonation map: A map showing the expected severity of earthquake ground motion, commonly in the form of contours of equal ground velocity or acceleration. The ground motion values are likely to be achieved at a specified level of probability (for example, 10%) over a specified period of time (typically 50 years).

Seismogram: The record made by a *seismograph*.

Seismograph (also **seismometer**): An instrument that records vibrations of the Earth, especially earthquakes.

Seismologist: A scientist who studies earthquakes or the structure of the Earth's interior from natural and artificially generated *seismic waves*.

Seismometer: See *seismograph*.

Shear wave (also called **S wave**): A type of *seismic wave* that is propagated through the Earth by a shearing motion, with oscillation perpendicular to the direction of travel. Shear waves can only travel through solids.

Shield: A large area of *Precambrian* rocks forming the geologically stable core of a continent (e.g., Canadian Shield). Shields are surrounded and overlain by younger rocks.

Slump: A type of *landslide* in which a mass of rock or *sediment* moves downward and outward along a curved slip surface.

South America plate: One of the large *plates* that forms the shell of the Earth. It includes South America and part of the South Atlantic Ocean seafloor. See pages 21 and 23.

Sovanco fracture zone: The *transform fault* connecting *Juan de Fuca* and *Explorer Ridges*. See page 30.

Spreading ridge (also called **spreading centre**): The growing edge of a *plate*, which is coincident with a *mid-ocean ridge*.

Stratigraphy: The study of *sediments* and *sedimentary rocks*.

Strike-slip fault: A *fault* along which rocks have moved laterally or horizontally past one another. See *transform fault*.

Subduction: The process of one crustal *plate* descending beneath another.

Subduction earthquake: An earthquake caused by the sudden slippage of one crustal *plate* over another at a *subduction zone*. Subduction earthquakes can be very large, up to magnitude 9.5.

Subduction zone: An elongate, narrow portion of the Earth's *crust* where one *plate* descends at an angle beneath another. Most subduction zones coincide with deep ocean trenches.

Submarine canyon (also **submarine valley**): A steep-sided trench or valley crossing the *continental shelf* or *continental slope*, resembling river-cut canyons on land.

Surface wave: A *seismic wave* that travels along the surface of the Earth.

Temblor: Shaking and vibration at the surface of the earth resulting from underground movement along a fault plane or from volcanic activity

Terrane: A distinctive, fault-bounded body of rocks of differing composition and geological history from adjacent terranes. Many terranes are thought to have been accreted, or added, to a continent at some time in the geological past (see *plate tectonics* and *seafloor spreading*).

Thrust earthquake: An earthquake caused by the sudden movement of rocks on a *thrust fault*. The rocks above the fault move upward or over the rocks beneath the fault.

Thrust fault: A generally low-angle *fault* along which rocks above the fault have moved upward and over rocks below the fault.

Tidal wave: See *tsunami*.

Transform fault:vA *strike-slip fault* along which a mid-oceanic ridge forming the boundary between two *plates* is offset.

Triple junction: A point that is common to three *plates*.

Tsunami: A series of waves produced by a major disturbance of the ocean floor, most commonly a submarine earthquake, but also a landslide, volcanic eruption, or meteorite or asteroid impact. Incorrectly referred to as a *tidal wave* – tsunamis are not tidal.

Turbidite: A layer of *sediment* deposited by a *turbidity current*. Most turbidites consist of sand and silt.

Turbidity current: A dilute mixture of *sediment* and water that flows at high velocity down an underwater slope and out along the floor of a lake or the sea. Turbidity currents deposit layers of sediment called *turbidites*.

Volcanic arc: A chain of volcanoes located inboard of, and parallel to, a *subduction zone*.

Volcanic ash: Fine fragmental volcanic material deposited during an explosive volcanic eruption. The average particle diameter of ash is less than 4 mm.

Wadati-Benioff zone: A dipping zone of earthquakes within the upper *mantle*, which coincides with a subducting *plate*. It is named in honour of seismologists Kiyoo Wadati and Hugo Benioff. Wadati-Benioff zones extends to depths of about 700 km beneath the Earth's surface.

Wrangellia: A large block of the Earth's *crust*, comprising Vancouver Island, the Queen Charlotte Islands, parts of the southeastern Alaskan archipelago, and parts of the westernmost British Columbia mainland. Wrangellia includes a wide variety of rocks that formed in oceanic settings at distant latitudes and that became attached to North America about 100 million years ago.

Wrench fault: A nearly vertical *fault* along which rocks have moved horizontally. Also called *strike-slip fault*.

Acknowledgments

THE AUTHORS ACKNOWLEDGE support and technical assistance provided by their colleagues, especially John Adams, Brian Atwater, John Cassidy, Herb Dragert, Roy Hyndman, Robert Kung, Stephane Mazzotti, Taimi Mulder, Garry Rogers, Kaz Shimamura, and Kelin Wang. Roy Hyndman made many helpful suggestions for improving the scientific and technical aspects of the book. Robert Kung created the DEM image used on the front cover.

The publishers, Glenn and Joy Woodsworth of Tricouni Press, provided much encouragement and support. David Woodsworth gave the manuscript a superb final check and proofreading.

The Geological Survey of Canada (Natural Resources Canada) supported Bob Turner's work on the project, and the Canadian Geological Foundation and Simon Fraser University provided grants that defrayed costs of manuscript preparation.

Photo and *Figure Credits*

The following people and institutions supplied illustrations. Numbers refer to pages.

Alberni Museum 55

C. Arnold 65 (top)

Brian Atwater 62 (upper right), 78, 85, 92, 93

Stein Bondevik 82

Caltech Institute Archives 41 (bottom centre)

Gary Carver 52

Alexis Clague 200

John Clague 80, 87 (bottom), 88 (top right), 104, 107, 121, 151 (bottom), 170, 171

Mark Cloos 88 (top left)

A. Dolgoff 39

DigitalGlobe 134

Earthquake Engineering Research Institute 56

Emergency Preparedness Canada 165

Environmental Systems Research Institute 23

Sigrid Federovich 83 (centre)

Fisheries and Oceans Canada, Institute of Ocean Sciences 139

Richard Franklin 200

V. K. Gusiakov 145 (left)

Graham Harrop 128

Henry Helbush 136

Ethan Hemphill-Haley 83 (top)

M. Hopper 166

Roger Hutchinson 112

Insurance Bureau of Canada 165

Donna Jones 86

Helen Lambourne 62 (upper left)

E.V. Leyendecker, National Bureau of Standards 65 (middle, bottom)

Donald Miller 142, 143

R. Milstein 87 (top)

Natural Resources Canada, Geological Survey of Canada 15, 40 (bottom), 41 (top), 53, 71, 74, 88 (bottom), 96, 98, 99, 109, 118 (bottom), 163

National Information Service for Earthquake Engineering, University of California, Berkeley 142, 143

Alan Nelson 88 (middle)

John Pallister 25 (top left)

Garry Rogers 34

Kenji Satake 90, 132

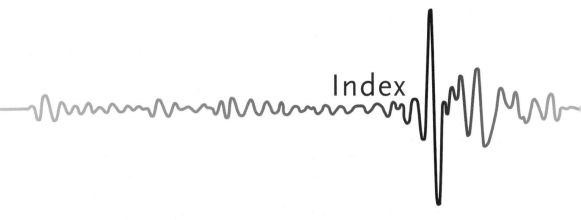

Index

Many terms used in this book are defined in the glossary, beginning on page 183. The glossary pages themselves are not included in this index.

About the Authors

John Clague is a Professor in the Department of Earth Sciences at Simon Fraser University. John's research interests are Ice Age geology, climate change, and hazardous natural processes, including earthquakes, tsunamis, floods, and landslides. His other principal professional interest is improving public awareness of earth science by making relevant geoscience information available to students, teachers, and the general public. John is a Fellow of the Royal Society of Canada and former President of the Geological Association of Canada. He lives in West Vancouver with his wife Alexis.

Chris Yorath is a geologist who, for 30 years, worked for the Geological Survey of Canada conducting research in the Canadian Arctic and western Canada, both on and offshore. He has authored over 130 papers and, since retirement, has published several popular books on various aspects of the geology of western Canada. Chris lives with his wife Linda on the Saanich Peninsula, north of Victoria.

Richard Franklin is a Victoria illustrator and graphic artist. His work has been widely published, and he has won numerous awards for both his scientific illustrations and exhibited art works.

Bob Turner is a scientist with the Geological Survey of Canada in Vancouver. He works to inform communities across Canada about their landscapes, water resources, changing climate, hazards, and environment (see www.geoscape.nrcan.gc.ca). He is co-author of the book *Vancouver, City on the Edge, Living with a dynamic geological landscape* and winner of the Geological Association of Canada's award for earth science education. Bob is currently Mayor of Bowen Island, where he lives with his wife Rosemary.